A Spiritual Aeneid

Ronald Arbuthnott Knox

Must Have Books
503 Deerfield Place
Victoria, BC
V9B 6G5
Canada
trava2911@gmail.com

ISBN: 9781773236797

CONTENTS

PREFACE

THIS book is a religious autobiography. The matter of it is not original, and (I thank God) the conclusion of it is not original either. But, so long as minds differ, there must always be some difference in the most hackneyed of pilgrimages, as the pilgrims compare notes at the Confessio.

I have tried to avoid all references that could be damaging to anybody but myself; if and where I have failed, I must take this opportunity to ask forgiveness. The publishing of autobiographies by the obscure is always, in any case, a target for criticism; but even obscure things have an interest; let us call it an autobiology. And before you say " self-advertisement "—think, what a bad advertisement.

In explanation of the Aeneid-*motif* which runs through the chapter-headings and parts of the book, I had perhaps better give the key to a somewhat obvious set of symbols. Troy is undisturbed and in a sense unreflective religion; in most lives it is overthrown, either to be rebuilt or to be replaced. The Greeks are the doubts which overthrow it. The " miniature Troy " of Helenus is the effort to reconstruct that religion exactly as it was. Carthage is any false goal that, for a time, seems to claim finality And Rome is Rome.

A SPIRITUAL AENEID

I

Me si fata meis paterentur ducere vitam
Auspiciis, et sponte mea componere curas,
Urbem Trojanam colerem.

NOT very long ago the Archbishop of Canterbury,
animadverting upon the varied religious experiences of a certain free-lance Bishop, described
them as "an episcopal Odyssey." The phrase is
wanting in aptness, when it is remembered that, wherever your Odyssey takes you, it must involve coming
back home at the end of it. I have dared to take my
title from a poem even richer in associations. For an
Aeneid involves not merely coming home, but coming
home to a place you have never been in before—one
that combines in itself all that you valued in the old
home with added promises of a future that is new. In
an Aeneid, as in an Odyssey, you may be driven from
your course ; but, to crown the sense of adventure, in
an Aeneid you do not even know where your port lies ;
you are bidden

Ausonium, quicumque est, quaerere Thybrim ;

you must make experiments, hark back to beginnings,
throw yourself upon a celestial guidance. Nor is it, as

B

in an Odyssey, the thought of familiar scenes and remembered faces that hurries you on when you are
tempted to linger, it is a mere sense of mission, imperiously insistent, that inflames your discontent :

Cunctus ob Italiam terrarum clauditur orbis.

And if in the course of this book I quote too freely, as
I have quoted just now, from the poem which is its
title, it is because the Aeneid travelled with me in the
last two months before the end of my journey, and I
read it, as Christians used to, with something like a
demand for spiritual comfort.

It is not easy for one who has abandoned a point of
view largely inspired by Catholicism in order to become
a Catholic to explain, or even to describe, how he came
to change his attitude. Let him set down as fairly as
he may the motives or the reasonings which once led
him to think otherwise ; Catholics (unless they have
encountered the same experience) will still fail to
appreciate how he ever managed to hold opinions so
self-contradictory ; and Anglicans, noting jealously
small differences between his previous and their present
position, will shelter themselves behind the retort of
the tadpole in Stevenson's fable : " Just what I
thought ; you never were an Anglican." Moreover,
from what point of outlook is such a writer to make his
retrospect ? From the valley of humiliation, or from
the hills beyond ? If he sets about his task immediately after his reception, the rival considerations are
all too fresh in his memory, and he may miss the wood
for the trees : if he delays the process he will (unless he

has Newman's accuracy and sympathy of mind) inevitably fall into the opposite error ; he will lose the true perspective, turn all the greys to black or white, produce, in short, a fancy picture.

To avoid the pitfall last mentioned, this book was begun in the week after its author was received. And none too soon ; for the mere prospect of the change had already begun to distort his memories of a former self—did he really support that paradox ? Did he honestly feel justified in that equivocal situation ? A friend, writing to me when he was finding his way out of that wilderness period which precedes conversion, and I was finding my way in, gave me a parallel which I cannot resist appropriating here. A man (he said) who once regarded but has now ceased to regard the Anglican Communion as the true Church (or part of it) is like a man who has woken up in the morning and, with the drowsy credulity of the half-awake, mistaken a pile of bed-clothes for a polar bear. The next moment he has seen it in a fresh light ; and now, turn his head or close his eyes as he may, he cannot reconstruct the lost impression, or see anything there beyond a pile of clothes. The application is easy. A month, a week, a day or two ago you found in the Church of England what you wanted ; to-day, with the same mental and spiritual apparatus, you torture yourself in the vain effort to recapture the lost angle of vision. This is not conversion. More than two years before I was actually received, the polar bear was gone beyond recall. And so, with two years of distance in between, I may even now be false to my earlier perceptions, and turn what is meant to be a candid document into a tract.

I do not want to write a tract. There are already plenty of such tracts abroad, and if they leave gaps, it is not for me to fill them. I am writing a history. The process of coming to believe in particular doctrines and then coming to change your view is not, in real life, a strict logical process, with *ergo's* and *distinguo's* for its milestones. Your religion builds itself up you know not how ; some habits of thought stepped into unconsciously, others imbibed from study, others acquired by prayer. And beyond that, the whole complex of your psychology, moulded by innumerable influences not merely religious, predisposes you this way or that ; your mental outlook, though it does not alter the facts, does condition the ways in which you come to appreciate them. I want, therefore, not to register the various " positions of my mind," but to trace the whole history of my mental background ; I want to make a present of myself to the psychologist. Let him burrow among my data, and pounce triumphantly upon my characteristic intellectual perversions ; I am only concerned to give him a faithful account. I do not mean that religion is a matter of temperament. God knows, I do not think my own conversion was temperamental. But if you put temperament altogether outside your reckonings, the whole human value of your document is lost.

I must not end this unconscionable preamble without a word or two in explanation of the terms I mean to use. When I say " Catholic," I mean what Anglicans call " Roman Catholic " ; I use the word so, not with any desire of treading on Anglican corns, but because, if I did otherwise, it would seem intolerably pedantic to those of my own religion. By way of compensation, I do not apply the term " Protestant " to all non-Catholics—to anybody, indeed, except those who would welcome it ; I apply it to those who protest not only against the specifically Roman claims, but against much in the structure of religion which the Greek Orthodox Church preserves; much, indeed, which was preserved by Martin Luther. The term " High Church," now grossly dissociated in the popular mind from all it was invented to describe, shall appear in these pages only under strict surveillance, chained to a quaternion of inverted commas.

.   .   .   .   .   .

I was born in 1888, the youngest of six children. My mother died when I was quite young ; and during that period of which I have anything more than scattered recollections—between the ages of five and eight—I spent the greater part of the year, with a brother a little older than myself, in a country rectory under the care of my father's mother, brother, and sisters. I cannot imagine circumstances better calculated to impress the mind with that form of Protestant piety which the modern world half regrets, half derides, as " old-fashioned." It has external marks—a strong devotion to and belief in Scripture ; a careful observance of Sunday ; framed texts, family prayers, and something indefinably patriarchal about the ordering of the household. It is easy to make capital out of such exterior manifestations ; and those who, having been brought up in such surroundings, have subsequently changed their views, are often at pains to ascribe all their later developments to a sense of revolt from a system described as sombre and inhuman ; Mr. Gosse early indoctrinated with Calvinism, Mr. Wells suffering under the terrors of a dæmonological nurse, are pictures which are supposed to present themselves as a nightmare to their more liberally educated readers. I suspect in all this a merely literary falsity of retrospect : certainly in my own case, apart from any question of piety, candour compels me to admit that I neither then found, nor have since managed to persuade myself that I found, anything repulsive or frightening in such a religious atmosphere. Hell was part of those beliefs, like death ; neither death nor hell dwells with any morbid fixity in the mind of a normal child. Rather, the personal love which God devotes to us, the ever-surprising miracle of His Redemption, the permanent ease of access to the glorified Saviour—these are the central characteristics of Evangelical devotion, and these its formative influences.

Was my childhood blighted ? I was assured, indeed, that the heart of man was desperately wicked— was that quite untrue ? At least, it was only the preface to the story of atoning grace ; at least there was hope in that message for the greatest of sinners. I suppose the most successful vehicle of such impressions to me, as to most people, was a series of familiar

hymns—chiefly, to me, " There is a Green Hill far
away." Yet with an odd sense that it was vulgar (as
if that mattered !) I always refused my homage to
Moody and Sankey's collection, only making a solitary exception in favour of " There were Ninety and
Nine." Redemption was a clear message to me : for
the rest, I believed that I was continually under the
eye of a watchful God, just in exacting punishment ;
but I do not think that the consciousness either
weighed me down or encouraged scrupulosity.

Not much in that early training was specifically
Anglican. Personal holiness I learned to admire from
precept and example ; doctrine did not consciously
figure. My brother and I got our Church Catechism
by heart as far as the sacramental section, and then
were promoted to the memorising of the Thirty-nine
Articles of Religion ; but I cannot remember carrying
much away from this latter exercise except a sneaking
affection for the sounding titles of those " uncanoni-
cal " books of Scripture we never heard read : " Bel
and the Dragon," " The Song of the Three Children,"
" The History of the Maccabees "—what guilty suggestions of hidden romance the words contained for
me ! But this is digression : I do not think that at
this time, apart from a familiar acquaintance with the
Book of Common Prayer, I imbibed much Anglicanism.

Of Catholicism as an existing fact I was only dimly
aware. It was a fact to be mentioned in bated breath
and with shakings of the head. It had, indeed, in-
truded itself into my family in two ways of which I

could not but be aware. My grandmother's sister had long before been received into the Church—one of the earliest letters of welcome I had was thus from an unknown cousin, Fr. David Arbuthnott—and as I bore her married name I must have heard something of her history. Further, my grandfather's parish had been that of Exton, where he wrestled manfully yet lived in courtesy with a Catholic lord of the manor— only a few months before my conversion this was recalled to me by meeting Lady Nora Bentinck, who could remember and admire my grandfather—and thus Catholicism was even to be imagined in connexion with our own quiet countryside. I think I looked upon it at that time as something highly aristocratic and at the same time secretly yet self-evidently wicked. But it only hung on the remotest bounds of my childish horizon.

On the other hand, Catholicism as a factor in history was very real and very abominable to me. Protestantism has, I suppose, been instilled into English people of education not so much by those infant catechisms in which an earlier generation delighted, nor even by the solidly one-sided picture which is still given of the Reformation in all early histories, as by a single book—*Westward Ho!* Nothing else binds up quite so successfully the cause of England's greatness with her loss of the Catholic Faith. I never read this book till much later, but I read many containing the same moral, and I came to assume, as all normal non-Catholic boys assume, that because the Reformation was successful it was therefore right.

Treason doth never prosper. What's the reason?
For, if it prosper, none dare call it treason—

There was never a more piercing analysis of English historical methods. The losing side is wrong, because it lost ; William of Normandy was a patriot, Philip of Spain a tyrant. The Reformation may be cherished by its devotees because the fires of Smithfield failed ; it is recommended to the hearts of Englishmen because the hangings at Tyburn succeeded. For, as a race, we pay our principal homage to the *fait accompli*.

I should say, then, that my historical views were as much coloured on this subject as those of most English boys—not more so, in spite of family traditions. But there is one exception, not indeed in the elementary histories, but in the novels of adventure, to this rule that the losing cause is wrong. A referendum in almost any collection of small boys would produce a vote in favour of, not against, the Stuart dynasty. Chiefly, I suppose, owing to Scott and Stevenson, this saving glimpse of the gloriousness of failure has been left to keep us all from pure materialism. In my own family, the " Cavalier " and " Roundhead " parties were equally divided at first ; I had embraced the latter cause chiefly, I think, because my hair hung straight, and I envied my brother's curls. At a sensational moment, for what reason I cannot remember, I played traitor to the standards of Dunbar and threw in my lot with the monarchy.

This *fin de siècle* loyalty never quite left me. Not, indeed, that I was ever in a serious sense a political Jacobite ; when I argued at the Oxford Union that the

Stuarts were the pioneers of Socialism I was conscious of paradox, and no one was more surprised than myself when, in commenting kindly on my conversion, the *Daily News*, my own breakfast organ, described me as " a Tory of the Tories," and the *Westminster Gazette* speculated whether I was anxious to put Prince Rupprecht of Bavaria on the throne. But I did naturally join, at Oxford, the ranks of those Anglicans who look upon the White King as a martyr for episcopal religion ; and of the effect of this atmosphere I shall have more to say later. But the thing went deeper than that : my sympathy for the lost cause of the Stuarts, combined with the sympathy I learned at Eton for " the sorrowful King " whose name closes the Lancastrian dynasty, did predispose me to an attitude of mind which is for reversing the judgments of history : I have always taken a Catonic pleasure in the defeated cause, and set my head against the stream. I am not here priding myself on the chivalry of such an instinct ; I am only suggesting that it is open for anybody to find here the cause, or the first symptom, of that readiness to defend the indefensible with which critics have frequently credited me.

Another remembered habit of those very early years I put on record because I found myself here to be in great company, when I last read Newman's *Apologia*. As a child, I often imagined (I must be pardoned for clothing my feelings in grown-up language) that the people round me were not separate centres of existence like myself, but were, so to say, a conspiracy of puppets, brought into my life from time to time and withdrawn

again by an agency which I did not doubt to be divine.
In a word, so far as occasional fancies can pass for
thought, I had lapses into subjective idealism of a
Berkeleian variety. Those, then, who say that Newman was in reality a sceptic all his days, may poke the
same accusation at me ; yet I have an eminently common-sense friend who also claims the experience.

Of another more dangerous mental trick I have still
more vivid recollections. It is common, of course, for
all children to tell imaginary stories to themselves or
to one another ; to fancy themselves in heroic situa-
tions, and fill the title-rôle of their romances. I used
to go further than this, and mentally construct my
autobiography, merely recording to myself my actual
movements at the time, in intervals of loneliness or
silence. " Then Ronnie went out into the garden . . ."
would be a typical beginning of such passages, never
spoken with the lips and never long sustained, but
conducive (I suppose) to self-consciousness. To make
of yourself an object external to yourself is to encourage in yourself habits of posing, of attitudinizing,
of speculating over the figure you cut before the world ;
it may be of advantage in the literary profession to
acquire such habits ; in life it is a permanent nuisance.
Children detected in the habit should certainly be
smacked.

.   .   .   .   .   .

Looking back upon my time at a private school, I
cannot resist the impression that I was rather a horrid
little boy. Perhaps everybody feels like that : it is a

period of life which lacks dignity and repose. But I cannot feel that those authors are right who attribute to this period heartlessness, absorption in trivial interests, the want of spiritual receptiveness. I am thinking especially of Mr. E. F. Benson's *David Blaize*, a book in which the admirable descriptions of a boy's thoughts really refer, I believe, to the public-school age, whereas some of them are supposed to belong to a private-school career. So far as devotion goes, I have a curious guide to my feelings at this time, from the circumstance of remembering the prayer, composed for myself, which I used to say daily on entering the school chapel. I hope I shall not be accused of impiety towards a former self if I set it down here. It ran :

" O God, I thank thee that thou hast heard all my prayers, and I pray thee that thou wilt forgive me for all my sins, and that the hymns may be nice, and that I may attend to-day, and ever hereafter. Amen."

Another reference to hymns—let me hasten to add that I am grossly unmusical ; barely capable of recognizing, and wholly incapable of reproducing, a familiar tune. But it is impossible to describe to people brought up on Catholic lines of devotion what an enormous part hymns play in the spiritual life of the ordinary not-very-religious Englishman. The Book of Common Prayer allows for no hymns, except a translation of *Veni, Creator* at Ordinations ; yet a Sunday service is not complete without three, four, or even five hymns : "The Voice that breathed o'er Eden " has more associations than any true part of the Wedding Service ; and, as we know, when English people are to meet death together, they prefer that the last earthly sound they hear shall be the music of " Nearer, my God, to Thee." I own that this tendency substitutes sentiment for devotion, but—sentiment is better than nothing. I can still hear " The Saints of God, their conflict past," as I heard it sung in the chapel of my private school, with a thunderstorm raging outside.

The reference to " attending " is also significant, for I was certainly anxious to the verge of scrupulosity about my frequent inattentiveness : and, as I did not then lay the blame for my shortcomings on any defect in the Anglican order of service, it ill becomes me to do so now. Certainly my religion—still without any tincture of Tractarianism—was quite real to me, nor was it an external matter only : I can remember tears of penitence after I had been punished for a fault, and, though the circumstances of an " interview with the headmaster " suggest the ludicrous, I have little doubt that then, if ever, I experienced full contrition. I do not think people with long memories and candid minds will find this description unnatural ; the age of reason brings a sense of responsibility, before adolescence overlays it with the temptation to spiritual carelessness. Anglican Bishops generally refuse to confirm (that is, incidentally, to admit to communion) boys of less than twelve years old—but I am wandering into controversy.

I cannot remember at all what the doctrinal teaching of my private school was like ; I imagine that it would be inspired by what ecclesiastical papers call " sound Churchmanship," but at such an age one does not acquire any particular devotion to doctrinal formulæ, and the services must have been ordinary enough. The only marked devotional habit I contracted here, in imitation of somebody, I suppose, was that of bowing my head whenever the holy Name was pronounced— in hymns, for example. I should explain that, whereas all or practically all Anglicans use this mark of respect in the recitation of the *Credo*, by an unintelligent reminiscence of the Canons of 1604, they have come to imagine that the habit is specially connected with the profession of belief — whereas the fact is that this happens to be the only time in the Prayer Book office when the holy name is pronounced while the congregation are standing. Tractarianism restored the wider custom ; but in adopting it I was certainly not conscious of any desire to "distinguish myself from my fellow-Christians." On the other hand, I remember that a lady who occasionally attended the chapel services (I think her daughter was engaged to one of the masters) was known to be " High Church " ; and I can still remember the *frisson* with which we used to watch the elaborate bow she made to the altar before leaving. Even to be the spectator of this gave me that guilty thrill I have described above in connexion with Catholicism ; it seemed to me at once very wrong and very attractive, probably for the simple reason that it suggested a secret tradition, a conspiracy somewhere afoot. I had a boy's love of mystery ; I belonged to a secret society of three—I suppose that, since my friend Mr. Cruttwell, afterwards of Magdalen, was received into the Church some years ago, it must now be regarded as automatically extinct—and embarked in the same company on the invention of a new and secret language, as boys will.. To have a secret at that age is to feel like a king.

And, talking of mystery, when did I, when does any boy, cease to believe in fairies ? Our faith in them is implanted in us by the same authority which teaches us the truths of religion ; they are quite as natural to us ; for myself, I had even had speech with a Manx boatman who had seen a Phenodore (or some such creature) with his own eyes. Yet at a given moment the belief seems to have slipped from me, and if I ever afterwards pretended to hold it, it was only by way of a pose. In other ways, I remained childish beyond my years, at least externally, and cherished my toys long after I might have been expected to abandon them ; the psychologist may take note, if he will.

One or two boys at the school were Catholics ; it never occurred to the rest of us to be interested in their beliefs. But I remember once hearing one of them taunted (in a fit of anger) with being a Papist ; I remember, too, quite distinctly the sense of embarrassment and horror with which we turned on the railer and kicked him, by way of inculcating manners. There was no question of tolerance ; we were simply in an agony of good breeding. When I left my private school at twelve years, I do not think that I was any more on the way to becoming a High Churchman than any English boy of that age.

I suppose I ought to mention here that the fatal germs of a literary bent had already discovered themselves in me. I began writing hymns at the age of six, but I am afraid, from what I can remember, that my efforts were deeply indebted to the work of previous authors. From hymnology it was a short step to nature poetry, to the grand drama, to all that one does write at eight years old. At my private school I proceeded to parody; perhaps more precociously, I began to write both Latin and Greek verse with what aid I could get from the Laws of Prosody at the end of the grammar; and a Latin play, in a curious variety of metres, was inflicted on my family by instalments. When I began to write Latin verse officially, I took kindly to it from the first, and the tendency was so far unchecked that to-day I can scarcely see a piece of English poetry without wanting to Latinize it. Educationalists will frown upon the idea that such a worthless facility could have any influence in the determination of the mind; for myself, I unashamedly believe Latin verse to be the first process (except perhaps Euclid, which we have abolished) that stimulates the mind to logical effort, in demanding that you should go behind the form of a sentence to get at its meaning. In any case, I gave hostages to the Muses, and laid myself open to whatever microbe it is that infects weak mortals with the literary temperament.

In closing this haphazard account of early tendencies, I must apologize for one obvious gap. I have spoken throughout of my education away from home; and the best part of anybody's education, particularly in matters of religion, inevitably comes from home influences. If I am silent about these, it is from a natural sense of piety and decency ; self-revelation cannot go all lengths. Accounting as they do for so much in the stuff and fabric of my religion, they cannot be discussed here, only acknowledged with a gratitude I can never cease to feel. The impressionist picture of my childhood must stand as I have drawn it.

II

ETON—PUBLIC-SCHOOL RELIGION

Nos alia ex aliis in fata vocamur :
Vobis parta quies ; nullum maris aequor arandum,
Arva neque Ausoniae semper cedentia retro
Quaerenda.

I CAME to Eton as a scholar in the autumn of 1900. Since it was in the course of my time at Eton that the attitude of my own mind changed, and my religious outlook became assimilated to the ideas of the Oxford Movement, I suppose I ought to unburden myself, here on the threshold, of my inevitable opinions on a subject stale from over-frequent treatment—I mean, ordinary public-school religion. I do not know that the religious atmosphere of the place differed much in my time from the description that is to be found of it in Mgr. Benson's *Confessions of a Convert;* if so, the account could easily be supplemented from Mr. Shane Leslie's *The End of a Chapter;* Mr. Leslie was my contemporary, and I wrestled with him for a form-prize in upper division. But, because I feel that public-school religion has had something less than justice done to it, I would like here to make some suggestions in moderation of the usual verdict before particularizing about any experiences of my own.

18

Critics of public-school religion really belong to two quite different groups—those who believe in the kind of religion which public schools try to instil, and regret their failure, in so far as they do fail, to instil it, and those who, believing in a different form of religion, whether Catholicism or an Anglicanism assimilated to it, tend to rejoice in the failure of the public schools, as becomes those possessed of an infallible remedy for such defects. I think, then, it should be said at the outset that public schools are trying to teach the sons of gentlemen a religion in which their mothers believe, and their fathers would like to : a religion without "enthusiasm" in the old sense, reserved in its self-expression, calculated to reinforce morality, chivalry, and the sense of truth, providing comfort in times of distress and a glow of contentment in declining years ; supernatural in its nominal doctrines, yet on the whole rationalistic in its mode of approaching God : tolerant of other people's tenets, yet sincere about its own, regular in church-going, generous to charities, ready to put up with the defects of the local clergyman. This religion the schoolmaster is under contract to teach ; it is left to him, if he be a sincere Christian, to attempt the grafting on to this stock of supernatural graces which it does not naturally develop—self-sacrifice, lively devotion, worthy reception of the Communion, and so on. That is the proposition.

Now, here is no question of what could or what could not be done if all school chapels were furnished and managed like (let us say) St. Alban's, Holborn. That is not the religion which the vast majority of parents

want, and the vast majority of schoolmasters personally believe in. To attempt the consolation of the
schoolmaster by pointing out to him the advantages of
an elaborate ceremonial and strongly Sacramental
doctrines, is like addressing a lecture on aviation to a
shipwrecked sailor treading water in mid-ocean :

> *Nihil iste nec ausus*
> *Nec potuit,*

it is not his business.

On the other hand, it is true that there is a sense in
which Catholicism can be taught, and ordinary Anglicanism cannot. For Anglicanism, generally speaking,
is not a system of religion nor a body of truth, but a
feeling, a tradition, its roots intertwined with associations of national history and of family life ; you do not
learn it, you grow into it ; you do not forget it, you
grow out of it. And if I were asked what was the best
way of perpetuating this tradition among boys between the ages of twelve and eighteen, I would say,
" Have a chapel of good architectural proportions,
decently decorated ; shorten the Anglican service for
daily use ; sing plenty of hymns, carefully selected ;
associate, as far as possible, the school with the school
chapel ; encourage the idea that its influence hallows
school friendships, consecrates school triumphs ; let
the preaching be patriotic, but not Jingo, about the
country, the Church, the school itself. Let confirmation be a public, not a hole-and-corner act ; spare no
effort to invest the Communion service with an air of
special aloofness and sanctity." It need hardly be
said that this is exactly what public schools do. And

the trouble is that it does not fail ; it succeeds. It succeeds only too well.

I know that there are rebels in public schools as in any other society, who really feel forced church-going to be an outrage and a tyranny ; they are quite few. The ordinary schoolboy grumbles at daily chapel-going because it is the habit of English people to grumble ; actually, he attends the services with equanimity, and on some occasions at least, such as Sunday evenings, is peculiarly receptive to impressions, chiefly of a sentimental order. The percentage of confirmed boys who present themselves for Communion, say, once a month would be totally impossible in an Anglican parish, an Oxford college, or any other Anglican institution not primarily ecclesiastical. The very awkwardness and embarrassment with which schoolboys "go up" to make their Communions is, viewed properly, a curious testimony to their appreciation of the occasion as a solemn one. It is true that even this voluntary attendance at a service so mysterious and so extraordinary can go on side by side with moral laxity and even gross sin ; religious impressions of this kind, still more the vague, sentimental impressions caused by popular sermons and favourite hymns, do wear off. But it is to be considered that the development of English boys of this class is slow, indeed, it is artificially retarded, and complete consistency of moral purpose is not necessarily to be expected ; it must be considered that, by the circumstances of their upbringing, they have no knowledge of any sacramental remedy for past sins, their efforts being devoted to "turning over a new leaf" from time to time. No sensible person can doubt that the average public-school boy of sixteen is more susceptible to religious influence than the average public-school man of fifty. Nor does the influence of the school chapel cease to have its effect when the boy has left ; rather, when he "comes down" he finds these more than ever a centre of inspiration. " I think one goes to early chapel, doesn't one ? " I have heard an old boy say on Saturday night, without the least approach to flippancy ; attendance at Communion is rated high when it is included among the things that "are done," as opposed to the things that "are not done" by Englishmen.

In a word, the selected youth of England is educated, exactly like Plato's guardians at the same time of life, not by intellectual study, but by traditions—δόξαι— implanted in the mind by suggestion, in which music and athletics play an important part. And their religious education is in this respect on a line with their secular education. But Plato points out that these traditions must "wash," must be capable of standing wear and tear. The public-school tradition is, in general, a dye that will wash ; its worst enemies do not deny that. But the corresponding tradition in religion does not, it must be admitted with regret, survive in most cases even the relatively gentle mangle of a university education ; the colours are running in the first year, by the third they have faded to something scarcely recognizable. It is not wholly a matter for wonder. You take away a boy of eighteen from an atmosphere in which religious worship has been an accepted feature of daily life, where all his emotions and aspirations have been, as far as possible, taught to twine themselves round an imposing building, consecrated perhaps by centuries of age and certainly by grateful memories of youth, where the masters (who, however despised, represented to him the grown-up world at large) were frequent chapel-goers of their own accord, and, at least in considerable numbers, communicants. You transfer him to a college where the chapel is probably not large enough to hold a full gathering of undergraduates, where chapel attendance is neither wholly compulsory nor wholly free, yet so intermittent that the music, such as it is, is relegated to Sundays, while the weekday office becomes dry and monastic : where the dons, *parci cultores et infrequentes*, set him little example of worship—but it is hopeless to seek words in which to express the difference. *Pauci quos aequus amavit Juppiter*, find in colleges such as Magdalen or King's an echo of the old illusion ; with these, I have observed, or perhaps fancied, the illusion dies harder ; but even here the Communion loses, for most people, its power of attracting their affections. The godly few betake themselves to favourite parochial shrines, *rari nantes in gurgite vasto ;* only an exceptionally popular evening preacher claims a real congregation. The rest, hunted out by the Dean or obeying a vague interior sense of decorum, " keep " a chapel at intervals.[1] All this is not simply

[1] " Here I am, *keeping* an Armageddon," a friend in the first of the new armies wrote to me from the Front. The use of the word here sufficiently illustrates the feeling of *noblesse oblige* with which undergraduates " keep " chapels.

the isolated experience of an unsuccessful college chaplain. I seemed to find all college chaplains agreed upon the difficulties here described ; nor can they be suspected here of merely professional pride, for there is no class of men so keenly alive to one another's defects.

When our hero goes out from the university into the wide world, his case is even worse. The churches in the immediate neighbourhood of his provincial or suburban home do not recall—how should they ?—the glories of his school chapel. A boy brought up at Downside finds himself at home in a hideous little mission church full of gimcrack images, because his religion has taught him to fly to the centre of things, and neglect the differences of external circumstances ; the Anglican has let his religious ideas be bound up with accidental conditions and local associations, and, though now and again a familiar chant may bring a lump into his throat, those conditions and those associations are not reproduced in the trim Mobraism of St. Matthias' Wherever-it-is. The Catholic knows a priest for a priest ; despises the man, it may be, but acknowledges his office, whatever his lack of personal attractions. The Anglican boy has very likely looked up to one particular schoolmaster as an oracle, drawn inspiration from him, and even " talked things over " with him ; but the public-school-and-university man he sees officiating at St. Matthias' is not the sort of man with whom he wants to talk things over : he may be a man and a brother, but he is neither father nor priest. If boys, as some critics suppose, disliked their school chapels, they might learn to like their parish churches. It is precisely because they like their school chapels that the parish church seems to them flat and stuffy and inadequate to the worship of God.

But (it may be argued) it is all very well to say that Anglicanism is not learnt as a lesson but caught like an infection, not imbibed but inhaled through the pores ; why, in that case, do I (" Paterfamilias " of the local evening paper) pay to have my son educated in " Divinity " two hours in the week ?   Why, if Catholics can propagate their errors with such success in the mind of youth, cannot the sober Anglicanism I love be taught to my son as Divinity ?   Why is Monday morning devoted to the barren scenes of Israel's wanderings, the waste waters sailed by itinerant Apostles ?   Why (in short) cannot the schools teach religion instead of theology ?

The answer is, I am afraid, that although the Anglicanism of Hooker and the Laudian divines, based carefully on Scripture and tradition, was capable of being worked out as a system and might be boiled down into a penny catechism, the Anglicanism of to-day, except where it is expounded by people definitely under the influence of the Oxford movement, simply does not possess enough of fixed background to allow of its being intelligently yet authoritatively taught. The nature of God, the position and destiny of man, the meaning of terms such as " soul " and " spirit "— fundamental doctrines such as these, with no suggestion of " Romanism " about them, are subjects on which expert Anglicans would pronounce variously, and non-expert Anglicans, if they could help it, would not pronounce at all. The idea of some schoolmasters I have known being called upon to teach such doctrines according to a syllabus is not within the bounds of moral possibility.

On the other hand, the exposition of the Bible as a book, or rather a series of books, the imparting of a little knowledge about some of the greater saints, such as Augustine or Francis, the teaching of a little Church history, however inadequate they may be, to supply the gap left in the religious upbringing of youth have a perfectly reasonable justification. Such knowledge forms part of a general education. Even a person with no religion ought to be able to locate some of the more famous texts of Scripture, ought to know that there was an Arian heresy and a council at Nicea, ought to be capable of distinguishing between the two Saint Augustines : his whole reading of literature, of history, even of newspaper articles, becomes at one point unintelligent if he is not so instructed. The weak point in the schoolmaster's defence is not that he teaches Divinity, nor that he defends the teaching of it, but that he defends it on wrong grounds, as if Divinity were religion. Knowledge about religious subjects can be conveyed, with no injury to conscience, by a man personally unconvinced on religious matters.[1] If the teacher is a man of such sympathy or such religious genius that he can contrive to make the dry bones live, to fire the imagination and stimulate

[1] I am not, of course, referring here to elementary schools, where the teacher is bound to aim at producing practical religion.

enthusiasm for his subject-matter, by all means let
him do so ; but (Paterfamilias must clearly understand) that is not what he is paid to do, it is an extra.
Why must the world expect all its schoolmasters,
when it does not expect its doctors, dentists, and
solicitors, to be men of genius ?

I am afraid I have wandered very far ; in excuse, I can only plead seventeen continuous years
since 1900 spent among schoolboys or undergraduates. And now I must return to my own
experiences.

For over three years after coming to Eton (a period
including my Confirmation) I was without any tincture
of " High Church " doctrines. I think my faith must
have been lively rather than reflective, when I recall
the fervent prayers for rain I used to offer when I was
put down to play in junior matches (I had to act as
long-stop to a fast bowler, but even so I cannot now
justify my anti-social attitude in this matter). Yet I
can remember writing home to my father, I think
about this time, to ask for explanations of some term
in the Athanasian symbol—a document which, whether
from its plain-song setting or as a relief from the same-
ness of the order of service, was hailed by us boys
with a delight that would shock our modern Prayer
Book reformers. It was in Eton Chapel that psalm-
chants began to claim my affection, hitherto reserved
for hymn tunes ; especially those for *Exsurgat Deus*
and for *Benedic anima mea Domino ; Domine Deus
meus*. The psalms themselves contributed attraction
to, and derived it from, the effect of the music. Ser-

mons I learned, for the first time, to criticize ; that great event of Sunday morning (for in ordinary Anglican churches the sermon is the climax, not an interlude as it is at High Mass) was always the subject of candid discussion. The chief merit in a preacher was the absence of reference to the Old Etonian missionary bishop George Augustus Selwyn. The late Provost had too soft, the present Provost too echoing a voice to be fully audible from the collegers' seats : the present headmaster, who became master in college about the middle of my Eton time, was undoubtedly the favourite preacher of those days. There was no doctrinal instruction, apart from the " Confirmation jaws " delivered by the then Provost in the winter half : from what I heard and what I can remember I should suppose them to have breathed the spirit of Cranmer, rather than of Laud.

The incident of that period which was most calculated to impress the mind was a fire which broke out in one of the houses, involving the death of two boys. It is, perhaps, at this time of life that one begins to fear death, and I can remember a curious, impersonal effect of this fear upon my ambitions. I had come to look forward to the Anglican ministry as my natural career—it was very much in the family ; but the thought of attending people on their death-beds, which I had now discovered to be a part of the clerical duties, filled me with repulsion. At one moment I tried to square the matter in my own mind by nursing the hope that I might be one of the " conducts " or chaplains who sang the services in chapel ; surely the closing of dying eyes could be none of their business. My own incapacity for music, and the comparative tameness of this ideal for a life's work, do not seem to have occurred to me. Later, I definitely abandoned in my own mind the idea of taking orders, though I slipped into it again naturally from the moment when I began to be bitten with the Oxford Movement.

But I am inclined to think that this lowering or obscuring of my ambitions—for I had no definite aim by which to replace them—was to some extent incidental to a time of life when the spiritual pulse beats low : the time, as I have mentioned above, which the Anglican Bishops have selected as the right Confirmation age. Certainly it was at this time that I abandoned the practice of saying my prayers in the morning (though not in the evening). I have no excuse for this neglect, which continued almost, if not quite, up to the time of my going to Oxford. As far as I can remember, my prayers at this time were inclined to be selfish : I had become something of a " pot-hunter," as those boys were called who made a speciality of winning prizes, and I had few friends to take my interests outside of myself. The only memory I have of strong spiritual feelings in my first years at Eton is that of a violent, almost hysterical penitence when my place in the term's order was lower than it should have been ; I have no doubt it was salutary, but I am afraid the subject of my repentance was characteristic.

Of reading I did singularly little at this age, apart

from my ordinary work. That work was still classical. It is pleasant to remember that at the end of my second half I was for abandoning the classics and taking to science. An introduction to elementary chemistry had enamoured me of glass tubes, litmus paper, and all the properties of the fascinating pursuit. I suppose the reasoning of it must also have attracted me in so far as it was pure reasoning, for Euclid was from the first the only form of mathematics in which I could either secure any marks or take any interest. But the days of reconstruction were not yet, and my authorities were wise enough to dismiss the suggestion, only tentatively made, and refer me back to my elegiacs. I continued to write English verse for my own amusement, mostly of a light and scurrilous kind, though I must plead guilty to some very jaundiced epigrams hidden away in an old note-book : it is easy to be a Schopenhauer at thirteen. About the middle of my Eton time I began to write occasionally for the *Eton College Chronicle.*

It remains to recall what I can of my Confirmation. It is well known that this rite is treated in the Anglican Church as preliminary to First Communion, and it is understood that the preparation for it should include a good grounding in Church principles, combined with such appeal to the emotions and encouragement to penitence as will dispose the boy to assume solemnly the responsibility for the promises made in his name at Baptism. I was prepared by my classical tutor, the Rev. H. T. Bowlby, now headmaster of Lancing. Both his house and his " pupil-room " were well thought of by clericalist parents of widely different types ; to be giving religious instruction at the same moment to an Adderley and a Kinnaird demands a conscientious moderation, and I do not think that " Paterfamilias " himself could have found fault with the instruction we got at our " Sunday private." Confirmation classes must (though we were quite unconscious of this at the time) have been a still more exacting business. A single instance will show that the difficulty was not insuperable. In expounding the significance of the Communion, my tutor read to us and enlarged upon the description of a " corporate communion " in Kingsley's *Westward Ho*, which insists strongly on what is known as the " congregational presence " of our Saviour in the Sacrament. I cannot imagine a better way of encouraging boys to feel the sense of mystery and privilege about the rite, where justice forbade, even if conviction would have preferred, anything but a moderate Prayer Book view. From these Confirmation classes I certainly carried away the feeling that the Communion service was a high mystery, and to assume the communicant status involved a spiritual standard worthy of full Church membership. I always prepared carefully for my Communions out of Bishop Walsham How's book, which my tutor gave me at the time.

Since I have just mentioned *Westward Ho!* I think I ought to put on record here that it was from my tutor (though not in connexion with Confirmation classes) that I learned to admire, though only by extracts, a very different book—*John Inglesant*, by

John Shorthouse. I do not know whether the book is much known to Catholics, but it has a strong cultus among Anglicans as a religious romance, and it will appear again in these pages. (Readers of Mgr. Benson's *Confessions of a Convert* will remember that he, after leaving Eton, conceived an "absolute passion" for *John Inglesant.*)

There was moral exhortation too, chiefly centred, in conformity with the tradition which has selected this age for Confirmation, on the subject of purity. I do not want to enter into any discussion here on the controversy as to when boys should be warned about moral dangers, and to what extent: I only want to allude to one *canard*. Boys are apt to talk amongst each other as if the private conversation on moral matters which forms part of the preparation system was really a police precaution to enable masters to make discoveries about the moral tone in their houses. Boys would talk like that. But for myself, far from having any personal impression of the kind, I never met anybody who could give me evidence of a concrete case in which this seal of the semi-confessional had been abused.

I was certainly lucky in my tutor, who was not merely in orders, but was personally in sympathy with much of the Tractarian tradition (although, as I say, I cannot remember his giving me any teaching of which my father would have disapproved). Complaints are often made of the system by which housemasters, though laymen, "prepare" their pupils: this is not the real grievance. Some housemasters really believe in the Anglican position, some are merely conforming Anglicans. And the possibility of having his son prepared for Confirmation by a man who says, " I don't know if you believe in original sin, because I don't," is not one that would be readily faced by a conscientious follower of the Prayer Book. Fortunately, the modern tendency is to take doctrine out of the hands of the tutor and entrust it to a central authority—the headmaster himself, where he is n orders, and where numbers make the system possible.

Yet, whether or not supernatural religion is being less and less taught, I am afraid that it is being less and less assimilated by boys at school. For myself, I seem to have accepted a supernatural religion without trouble or speculation at this period. I can remember that the same master introduced us to the theory that the Books of Samuel (as the first two Books of Kings are called in the Authorized Version) were a collection of different accounts, with the incidents occasionally overlapping, put together not always with a skilful hand, and to Wolf's theory of Homer, according to which the Iliad was a collection of separate lays. The higher criticism of the Bible amused without disturbing me ; I did not greatly care whether it were verifiable or not. But the attack on the Iliad roused me to fury. As far as Wolf was concerned, the spirit of *Pascendi Gregis* descended on me and has never left me.

It is unprofitable to speculate upon might-have-beens, but it is only fair to my early religious educa-

D

tion to say that, under God, I think I should have gone up to Oxford as a believer and a regular communicant even if I had not come under the influences which are to be described in the next chapter :

Trojaque nunc stares, Priamique arx alta maneres.

III

ETON—A TRACTARIAN PERIOD

Da moenia fessis
Et genus, et mansuram urbem : serva altera Trojae
Pergama, relliquias Danaum atque immitis Achillei.
Quem sequimur? quove ire jubes? ubi ponere sedes?
Da, Pater, augurium, atque animis illabere nostris.

I WAS actually confirmed not at school but at Birmingham by my father, who was at the time Suffragan Bishop of Coventry. In the autumn of that year, 1903, he was translated to the See of Manchester.

It was at Manchester, on Christmas Day, 1903, that I read a book written (I was told) by an Anglican who had just become a Roman Catholic (actually, in that September). It was, of course, *The Light Invisible*, a collection of stories written by Mgr. Benson while he was still in the Church of England. I was induced to read it as the result of an argument in which, for the first time, I had been confronted with the usual contentions in favour of various Catholic doctrines and practices—the Real Presence, the Sacrifice of the Mass, etc.—and had attempted to controvert them with all the uninstructed zeal of a combative nature.

Now, there is nothing whatever in the book of a polemical character. It describes the imaginary ex-

periences of an old (Anglican) priest[1] who has a sort
of religious second sight, becomes conscious in moments
of illumination that there is a supernatural world
interpenetrating and intersecting with the world of
sense. He is not a mystic but a seer. Most people
find it an interesting book, but free from controversial
tendency. Later, when I was teaching at Shrewsbury,
I found that my predecessor had been reading it to his
form on Sunday afternoons. Yet, to me, that Christmas Day was a turning-point. It was the setting of
the book—the little chapel in which the priest celebrated, the terms in which he alluded to the Mother
of God, the description of confessions heard in an old
parish church—that riveted me even more than the
psychological interest. All that Catholic system which
I had hitherto known only distantly, felt as something
wicked and felt attracted to only because it seemed
wicked, now for the first time entered my horizon.
In a modern phrase, I was " up against it."

At the end of the next half I was to compete for the
first time, at the age of sixteen, for the Newcastle
Scholarship. This examination is mainly classical,
but there are three divinity papers, one of them on
Church History, which tell considerably in the final
award. It was not the Age of the Fathers that fanned
the flame Hugh Benson had kindled in me, it was Wake-
man's *History of the Church of England*. It is an
eminently respectable book, most definitely Anglican

---

[1] Mgr. Benson says the priest was not particularly meant to be Catholic or Anglican ; but when he hears confessions in an old parish church,
the patronage of which has come into " Catholic " hands, it is clear that
he speaks as an Anglican.

on the Reformation question, but inevitably tinged by the author's own sympathy for the Tractarians. Consequently, it leads up to the Oxford Movement as to a climax. Here is the fruit of the seed planted by St. Augustine and St. Thomas of Canterbury springing up irrepressibly after three centuries of blight. I read, and was carried off my feet ; I lived through the early struggles, followed breathlessly the story of *Tracts for the Times*, trembled for Newman, mourned for him as lost to the Church, and rose with the knowledge that somewhere, beyond the circles I moved in, there was a Cause for which clergymen had been sent to prison, a Bishop censured, noble lives spent ; a Cause which could be mine.. Newman's loss, profoundly as it stirred the imagination, impressed me only as a defection ; when I read Browning's *Lost Leader* I recognized him there. Occasionally a chill struck through me—was he right in thinking the *Via Media* untenable ? Once, a year or so later, in trying to revive the embers in my grate with a copy of the *Church Times*, I said to myself, " Let this be an omen." (I must confess that I frequently take omens, though I hardly ever follow them.) " If I can get this fire to burn, the Oxford Movement was justified ; if not, it was a vain effort." It was quite a sporting chance, the coals still glowed faintly. The fire went out slowly, and I rose cursing myself for my superstition. But, had I accepted the omen, I should not therefore have thought Rome right ; I should simply have thought the Oxford Movement wrong.

It will be seen that, so far, my new religious interests

were rather in the air ; they had form, but no content. I knew little of High Churchmen, what they believed, valued, or practised. All I knew of such movements during the time I was in Birmingham was that a reprehensible clergyman existed, Pinchard by name, who was given to walking about the streets in a cassock. I had no precise idea where his delinquency lay ; indeed, I conceived it vaguely as consisting in some heretical view about Mr. Balfour's Education Act. Now, the atmosphere of Catholicism had dominated my imagination, and the history of the Oxford Movement had awakened all that was latent in me of enthusiasm for lost causes. In order to fill out my impressions, to lend substance to my dreams, I consulted one whom I then knew very little, though I can since claim him as a friend. He, brought up at a Sacramentalist church, could think of nothing better to lend me than a book of a severely didactic character called *The Ritual Reason Why.* Here I read elaborate explanations of the mystical meaning symbolized by amices, incense, the sign of the Cross—read, and revelled in them. It must, I think now, have been a disgustingly ritualistic book, and its black-and-white drawings were not in the least calculated to fire a boy's imagination. But I had accepted the new freemasonry, and every symbol was sacred to me ; long before I had ever seen a ritualistic service I became a Ritualist.

This was in the summer of 1904. I cannot pretend to give an historical account of the small incidents that may have directed my mind in the next two years : I

will only try to put on record the chief ways in which
my new views made themselves felt.

First, then, I was a party man. I took in the *Church
Times* during the half, and revelled in its descriptions
of elaborate services; learned, also, which Church
leaders I was to look upon as allies, which I was to
treat doubtfully, which to anathematize. Argument,
at this time, I enjoyed more than most things; and
argue I did, with two of my acquaintances especially,
over the whole field of religion and polemics. Yet I
made very little effort to proselytize among my friends,
for the ideas were all in my own head; I could not
take people to a church I should have approved of
and say, " There ! there is the thing working." I
read a good deal in these two years, but singularly
little that touched religion ; poetry and the classics
were my preference. The present headmaster and
Mr. William Temple managed to inoculate me with
Browning ; I would sit up by a fire after lights were
put out learning Keats by heart. But my studies did
not often extend to theology. I read something of
Bishop Gore : he had been kind to me in Birmingham,
where he was my father's diocesan, and the mur-
murings of old-fashioned people who thought him
over-Liberal had not reached me. I think it must
have been at school that I bought his " Roman Catholic
claims" and Dom John Chapman's answer to it : not
because I felt unhappy, but because they were pamphlets of the moment. I set out to read them alternately chapter by chapter, but stuck at the end of the
first—I do not know which author was responsible.

My most solid theological achievement was Canon Moberly's *Atonement and Personality*, which I read mostly in a period of the afternoon at which boys in First Hundred might, as a substitute for mathematics, read what books they liked (of an improving kind) under the eye of a master. (I can still hear my next-door neighbour giggling over *A Tramp Abroad*.)

Yet I was beginning to acquire tastes, or rather hobbies, which no doubt reacted on me. One was a slight reading in and great devotion to the Gothic in architecture ; another, which fitted in with it, was an insatiable love of the pre-Raphaelites, whether Italian or Mid-Victorian[1]—the history of the latter group I once had at my fingers' ends. I had, and have, no vestige of artistic taste ; but the spirit of revival in Holman Hunt and Rossetti accommodated itself to the spirit of revival in Pusey and Neale ; the two movements were curiously grafted together in my mind. I was, indeed, a conscientious Goth, so far as architecture, vestments, etc., were concerned, up to the end of my undergraduate days.

I had few like-minded people to exchange opinions with. My chief ecclesiastical confidante was the then matron in college, to whom I am indebted for much salutary instruction and correction as well as sympathy. Boys (and there are not a few of them) who become infected, as I was, with religious "views" at school, need above all things a safety-valve ; if I had

---

[1] I see Mr. Alec Waugh says boys are not encouraged to read Rossetti or Swinburne. This is violently contrary to my own experience.

had nobody to discuss my ambitions with, the burden
of my secret might have had an unhealthy effect, and
I might have become morbid, fanatical, or unbalanced.
Among the kindnesses I had from her was an introduction which became interesting later. She had been
for some time a nurse under the Universities' Mission
to Central Africa, a mission which owes its whole
origin to Tractarian inspiration ; and when the Chan-
cellor of the diocese of Zanzibar came down to preach,
it was at her table that I met him. His commanding
presence was not what one associated with missionaries—a cassowary, you felt, would have looked twice
at him ; and his address, which was simple but strongly
sacramental in tone, added to the demand for my
youthful homage. But I could not know that it was
he who, as Bishop of Zanzibar, was to be one of the
protagonists in a Church controversy that shook the
British public as nothing of the kind had shaken it for
forty years, and led the British Press—*causas tanti
sciat illa furoris*—to smother him with anathemas.

At home my views were known, and doubtless regretted, but never led to the smallest discontinuance
of kindness on one side nor (I hope) of respect on the
other—certainly not of affection on either. I did not,
I think, till some time later, attend services in Manchester of a kind my father disapproved of. Nor did
I feel my position equivocal as the son of an Evangelical champion, for these were the days[1] of Mr.
Birrell's Education Bill, when my father would appear
on platforms side by side with Lord Halifax, and

---

[1] That is, the end of my time at Eton.

even Catholics can look back with gratitude on the
alliance—

Saevis, hospes Trojane, periclis
Servati facimus, meritosque novamus honores.

A fierce hatred of what was then called "Birre-
ligion" was my earliest political sentiment.

So much for my education as a partisan; I have
now to speak of its effect on my devotional practice.
So far as my evening prayers went, this made, at the
time, no difference whatever; except that on Saints'
Days mentioned in the Anglican Calendar I used, for
a time, to invoke the saint of the day while getting
into bed. I gave up the habit because I came to the
conclusion that my reasons for it were only superficial
and emotional, without intellectual basis; then, as
always, I dreaded the undue interference of emotion
in religion. I did, however, buy one or two religious
prints, which I hung up so as to say my prayers in
front of them. Later a very small crucifix was added
to the group. Sometimes I lighted joss-sticks in front
of these pictures, but more for gratification of the
senses than from any feeling that God would be pleased
with this Oriental homage. Once I bought and burnt
some candles. But a warning from a priest whom I
met in the holidays suppressed in me, very largely, the
unhealthy ritualistic instinct which boys often have.
I do not think it was ever part of my nature, for I cannot remember, when I was small, ever celebrating the
exequies of the dead mice, etc., that suggest such
fancies to other children.

After my "conversion" (for so I was accustomed

to think of Christmas, 1903), I used to communicate every Sunday. Early celebrations in chapel were in those days only fortnightly, and the odd weeks necessitated a visit to " the church down town " ; and those who say there is no religion at public schools should take note that on these occasions thirty or forty boys would regularly give up their " long lie " to attend its very ordinary Anglican ministrations. In this church I used to adopt some of the gestures of Catholicism, such as genuflecting and blessing myself ; in chapel I refrained, not from conscious accommodation, but from natural herd-instinct. In my last year I occasionally managed to communicate on week-days in the parish church.

I also came to attend regularly the services of preparation for Communion (with addresses) which took place several times a half on Friday nights in Lower Chapel. I thought then, and think still, that these services, where attendance (on the busiest evening of the week) was entirely voluntary, were the most real part of the religion there, although I believe the right of attendance at them was sometimes abused. Considering the respect in which they were held by the numerous people who went to them, it is very characteristic that in college the service was always referred to as a "beano," and among oppidans as "a night attack." The very nicknames were a sort of euphemism for something that sounded pious, too pious to be mentioned. Such, I suppose, is schoolboy reserve ; for myself, I will not call it irreverence.

As I say, I never haunted congenial churches even

in the holidays. I think I only once attended a service with " full ritual " before I went up to Oxford. Of Catholicism, *a fortiori*, I saw less. The only exception to this was a visit to Germany and Belgium with one of my brothers. We were there a fortnight, and (at my instigation) we investigated almost every church in Cologne, besides others at Treves, Strassburg, Heidelberg, Bonn, and Mainz ; we even crossed from Coblenz under the shadow of the Ehrenbreitstein to visit the pilgrimage church of Arenberg. In Ghent and Bruges we followed the stream of tourists from shrine to shrine. Yet we managed to see nothing of the High Mass in Cologne Cathedral, and my only other effort at Catholic worship was an unsuccessful attempt to follow the ceremonies of Benediction at the Jesuitenkirche with the aid of Mr. Athelstan Riley's admirable *Guide to High Mass Abroad*. (It sounds silly, but I had the misfortune to catch the words " *mea culpa, mea maxima culpa*," which suggested the Preparation, but were really part of Compline.) I carried away no definite impressions about Catholicism ; even Bruges failed to work the spell with which it afterwards caught me. I think the whole thing was so foreign that the eccentricities of the local religion affected me no more than those of the local diet. The chief relic of my visit was a small silver crucifix, which afterwards adorned first my walls, then my watch-chain, then my neck.

But, while I was thus indifferent to the quest of ritualistic spectacles, I developed during my last year at Eton an extraordinary fondness for attending Evening Prayer. Sometimes I would pursue it as far

as the " church down town," but, of course, I preferred
to have it sung, as it is daily, by the conducts and paid
choir in college chapel. On whole school days this was
impossible, but there are three half-holidays in the
week, and on these, at least during my last half, I must
have attended Evensong oftener than not. It was not
meant for the school, and it was the rarest thing to
find another boy at it. Only a thin sprinkling of pious
ladies formed the congregation. The service was an
ordinary cathedral service, and I was wholly unmusical. I had no great sense of devotion, rather one
of peace and regularity and contact with historic
things. Many of the Psalms, especially the Gradual
Psalms, I came to love. But—here is the tragedy of
the situation—the exercise seems to have acted as a
sort of Keeley treatment ; and during my last six years
as an Anglican I would, apart from the sense of duty,
never have troubled to cross the street in order to
attend Evening Prayer.

I have said above " contact with historic things."
For the chapel itself was to me intimately connected
with the memory of the pious founder, King Henry
the Sixth, to whose personality I had a singular devotion. Again, as in the case of King Charles I, it was the
misfortunes of my hero that endeared him to me ;
here was another lost cause to claim my sympathy.

> Scholars of Henry, keep the fame
> Of him, the sorrowful King, who came
> Within his realm a realm to found
> Where he might stand for ever crowned.

Certainly he does, and although his own chapel

never hears it, we in college were familiar with a hymn which begins with the somewhat un-Anglican address :

> Rex Henricus, sis amicus
> Nobis in angustia,
> Cuius prece nos a nece
> Salvemur perpetua.

To me the memory of the founder was a sacred trust, and I never entered Cloisters on my way to Hall without saying inwardly a prayer for his soul. At Oxford I helped to start a Celebration at Pusey House for Etonians on Founder's Day.

And there was another element in this feeling I had for him and for his chapel. It was dedicated, and the school was dedicated, to Saint Nicholas and Saint Mary. The founder was born on December 6th, Saint Nicholas' Day, just before the feast of the Immaculate Conception. Thus, although I did not ask for her prayers, I had a strong sense of the patronage of the Mother of God. Her name was part of our title ; her lilies figured on our coat of arms ; the blue of her robe you could see daily on the blazers of the Eight and the caps of the Eleven. And perhaps, after all, in the wide sympathies of her compassionate heart there is a special place kept for her children at Eton. I only know that it was the easiest thing in the world, on any of her feasts, to arrange for the singing at college prayers of that rather sentimental Ancient and Modern hymn which begins, " Shall we not love thee, Mother dear ? " And those who believe that schoolboys like strong, sensible hymns will be disappointed to learn that it was always sung with enthusiasm. But I am becoming, for Anglican readers, too fanciful ; for Catholic readers, too reminiscent. Let it suffice that, at a time when I hardly thought of her as differing in glory from the other saints, I already thought of her as having a special interest in me and a special influence on my life. *Prosit*, she seemed to say, *nostris in montibus ortas*.

I think I hear somebody suggesting that, for one who has just proclaimed his distrust of emotionalism in the religion, these last few paragraphs seem a trifle inconsistent ; was I not, after all, a sentimental schoolboy indulging myself by playing at the Catholic religion ? The inconsistency I admit ; my veneration for St. Mary of Eton was not based on any solid doctrinal ground. But to the accusation of self-indulgence I demur, because from the first an integral part of my new religion was a feeling for asceticism ; I wanted to make myself uncomfortable. The most definite form these ideas ever took was dictated by the occasion of a friend's illness. He went down suddenly with typhoid ; and I, with the feeling that I must somehow make myself useful, determined on fasting as a supplement to prayer ; I would eat nothing except bread and butter until his fate was decided. This abstinence was impossible on the rare occasions when I went out to meals with masters, but among my schoolfellows it passed simply as a criticism on the quality of the food provided for us, and they must have supposed that I made good by " socking " down town. The illness lasted nearly six weeks, during which my bread-and-butter rule was faithfully observed ; at the end my friend died. I can remember the perfectly businesslike way in which I returned to a more elaborate diet the same evening ; this was not heartlessness, for King David observed the same principle (2 Kings xii. 22). Another exercise of mortification I invented upon the same occasion was to pray for my friend with both hands held above the level of my head for a quarter of an hour or more ; this (which is not as easy as it sounds) is a practice I have sometimes returned to. All this did not in the smallest degree shake my belief in the efficacy of prayer, a doctrine which I remember defending to a friend (Charles Lister) soon afterwards.

Asceticism led me to another resolve of a more permanent character. I think I could still point to the precise place on "Chamber Stairs" where I knelt down at the age of seventeen one evening and bound myself by a vow of celibacy. The uppermost thought in my mind was not that of virginity : I was not fleeing from the wickedness of the world I saw round me. Without wishing to embark on a controversy, I must say here that (*pace* Mr. Alec Waugh) I believe it possible at an ordinary house in an ordinary school for an ordinary boy, though he may hear much obscene conversation and much scandalous gossip, to go through his school time without having the moral evils which sometimes lie beneath the surface, thrust upon his notice. I knew people who were by repute immoral ; the conventions of our society, as well as charity, demanded that I should give them the benefit of the doubt : I never heard a boy deliberately boast of his own sins. It was not, then, a sense of oppression about purity that influenced me. But at this time (as is common, I suppose, with many people) I was just beginning to form close and intimate friendships ; I was just beginning also to realize that in many cases such friendships were likely to be dissolved through circumstances of separation after leaving school. And, conscious for the first time how much my nature craved for human sympathy and support, I thought it my obvious duty to deny myself that tenderest sympathy and support which a happy marriage would bring. I must have " power to attend upon the Lord without impediment."

I have no notion, humanly speaking, whence these ascetic impulses came. I cannot remember that any of my reading up till then would have suggested them to me—there is little trace in *The Light Invisible* of that atmosphere of mortification which inspires so much of Mgr. Benson's later writing. The aspiration must, I think, have been self-sown, and, poor as is my record of self-denial since then, I think the doctrine of merit is the most lucidly obvious to me still of all the truths of religion.

It will no doubt be supposed, from what I have written, that I was a shy, reserved, unpopular sort of boy, much given to self-communing and morbid imaginings. I can only say that the exact contrary was the case. This was just the time at which I was blossoming out into a sympathetic friend and a tolerable companion. I knew everybody round me, I wasted endless hours in talking, I watched matches, ate cake, scamped my work like anybody else. I was only ex-

ceptional as regards literary ability. I had won a
Balliol scholarship a year earlier than I need have, and
I wrote constantly for the *Eton College Chronicle*, which
I finally edited, also once or twice for the *Cornhill* and
the *World*. Yet neither the scholar nor the poet in any
school story I ever read was anything but unpopular.
I was quite hopeless at all games; yet nobody ever
tried to " crush my originality " or " force me into a
mould," or do any of the harm public schools are
generally supposed to do in the case of unusual tem-
peraments. I was supremely happy, and accepted
everywhere at my own valuation as a very normal
Etonian : I was elected to " Pop " in the Michaelmas
half of my last year, when I should not have been so
ex officio (as captain of the school) till after Christmas.

Two incidents in my career won me friends, neither
of them through any merit of my own. Success makes
us acquaintance, but only misfortune gives us friendship. I was defeated by a friend (Patrick Shaw-
Stewart) when I was expected to get the Newcastle
Scholarship—that was the first incident. I remember
that I sat down and read the Book of Job straight
through by way of spiritual comfort. The consolation
offered me by two of the masters especially about the
meaning of failure had, I think, a permanent effect
upon me. I had already a fondness for lost causes, and
now I became distrustful of my own ambitions—what
better training could one have for following in the steps
of the Tractarians ?

This was not my last chance for the Newcastle ; but
in my last year, almost on the eve of the examination,

I went to bed with appendicitis. Here was the second incident, and I do not know that I ever tasted such publicity. Appendicitis was still thought serious in any case ; in my own case, I understood later, there was good chance of my not recovering, and for a time they did not like to operate. To be " prayed for in chapel " when you are captain of the school hardly occurs outside the school stories. I should say that the net effect of this chastening was less salutary, so overwhelmed was I with kindnesses which even now I blush to think of.

This illness also, I think, marks a stage in my religious development, not because it changed me, but because it brought me into touch with "advanced Churchmanship " at first hand. My nursing home lay between All Saints', Margaret Street, and St. Mary Magdalen's, Munster Square ; several of the nurses attended the latter, as did Mrs. Remanes and the late Dr. Oswald Brown, who often came to see me. One morning the Vicar celebrated in my room and gave me my Easter Communion. The Bishop of London also came, with characteristic kindness, both to see me and to celebrate for me. It is strange to me to reflect that, on the eve of my operation, when the Bishop asked me privately if I had anything on my mind, I failed to take the obvious hint, and this although I fully intended to go to Confession after leaving school. I suppose I was very weak in body, and Confession, which to a Catholic would have been a relief, presented itself to me as an unmanageable effort.

During my last half I am afraid I was something of a

nuisance to the authorities. Eton, I think, fosters contempt of law and reverence for convention—not altogether a regrettable tendency, for law is imposed from outside, while convention is democratic through and through. My literary efforts tended to scurrility—I mean, to " personalities " which were not everywhere appreciated. To have published a book of poems at that age is certainly a snare. God forgive me if I left any unkind memories, for certainly nothing ever did (or will, I suppose, in this life) give me such happiness as the end of my time at Eton. Tea in Sixth Form Passage on November afternoons, with your pores tingling from a hot bath ; sunny days when you sat on the low wall in front of chapel, or wandered out to watch cricket from the pavilion ; unintellectual acquaintances, vague satisfaction in boyish authority, a few treasured friendships, antiquity in the very air you breathed, yet youth all round you and within you, and the river flowing through it all to remind you of transcience and of eternity—*fulsere quondam candidi tibi soles.*

IV

BALLIOL—SECULAR INFLUENCES

Mantua, dives avis, sed non genus omnibus unum.

LEAVING Eton I felt definitely as a tragedy ; Oxford, in spite of its comparative freedom and its historic traditions, was always a very poor second best. Yet from the first I threw myself into the manifold life, or rather lives, of the place, with a fervour that puzzled my friends and occasioned justifiable misgivings to my tutors. I think it will conduce to clearness of view if I try to give some idea of the secular framework of my Oxford existence, reserving the question of my religious developments to a separate chapter.

First, then, I had my Eton friends, both in Balliol (an unusual number of them) and elsewhere ; Etonians, I think, keep more in touch at the Universities than people from most schools. At Balliol, we came in for a tradition bequeathed by earlier generations of Balliol men, and some of us, I must say, developed it ; its atmosphere was one of energetic rowing, hard drinking, plain dressing, occasional gambling, and unexpected because apparently unmerited academic triumphs. I cannot say that I was personally true to the type at its best or its worst ; I only mean that I was the friend of people who were. What the late Prime Minister called "the effortless superiority of Balliol men " did not make us altogether popular outside College ; nor, internally, did my friends avoid friction with the authorities. Yet we had friends outside, at Magdalen particularly and at University. Magdalen " afters," University smokers, and " Annandale " dinners stand out in memory as one element of the curious chaos in which I lived.

We Etonians were supposed to keep to ourselves unduly, but personally I drifted into a second circle in College where other schools were represented equally —Rugby, Marlborough, Clifton, Rossall, Stonyhurst. It was in this circle chiefly that my intellectual appetite was whetted and my philosophic views formed by argument ; here, also, that much of my most agreeable leisure was spent, eating interminable teas in winter, and dining in punts on summer nights by backwaters of the river.

Thirdly, I was early marked down for a politician of the Oxford type and a speaker who could be depended upon to support any view in any debating Society. My evenings were a riot of discussion, my mantelpiece smothered in fixture-cards ; besides belonging to the Union, the Oxford Church Union, and the Christian Social Union, I was a member of the Arnold, Devorguilla, Fabian, Jowett, and Decalogue Societies, the Canning, Orthodox, and Shaftesbury Clubs, the Tariff Reform League, and the group known as *De Rebus Ecclesiasticis*. One acquainted with the Oxford of the day will realize that this list implies considerable elasticity of the political conscience, and indeed I

needed it.   On the one side, Charles Lister, whom I
knew best among the people who had come up from
Eton with me, was a strong Socialist, so was my brother
at Trinity ; I supported Charles Lister in numberless
progressive activities, and was prevailed upon by him
to join the Fabian Society, whose basis (at Oxford) was
then more economic and less political than it became
since. Socialism, at the time, enjoyed some popularity
in orthodox Church circles ; a reforming enthusiasm
in politics went easily hand in hand with traditionalism
in religion : Charles Lister allowed me to drag him to
church, and I allowed him to drag me to meetings ;
nor did either of us thereby do any violence to conscience.

On the other side, I suppose partly because I shared
my father's well-known views on religious education,
I was equally hailed as a Conservative, and elected a
member of the Canning. *Nocles cenaeque deum !* It
was a wonderful assemblage. Four of us, if not five,
professed ourselves " Tory Socialists," including Mr.
Neville Talbot, whose wavering conscience (for he was
becoming a thorough Radical) I remember trying to
reconcile by sophistical interpretations of the Club
oath. Lord Eustace Percy was the chief representative
of reaction ; Lord Wolmer, as secretary, made manful
efforts to keep us all in tow. As I say, I had to vote
Tory on Education, and I was willing to give a rather
nominal assent to the doctrines of Tariff Reform :
this sufficed, for it was a moment when Toryism was
developing from a church into a creed.

At the Union, where I made numerous other political friends, wasted invaluable hours, ran through the course of offices, and became President at a comfortably early date, I passed chiefly for a Conservative, though it was not necessary for a speaker to belong consistently to any party. I voted No Confidence in the Government with Mr. Wyndham, Home Rule with Mr. Redmond, Socialism (dare I admit it ?) carried off my feet by the eloquence of Mr. Philip Snowden. Toryism still had hopes of me, and both Mr. Wyndham and Sir F. E. Smith urged me to abandon my clerical ambitions and embrace politics as a career. It was a confused position, certainly : . I have canvassed for Mr. Steel-Maitland at Southam, and helped to found a Trade Union at Banbury. But (and this is the reason for my dwelling on the subject) I do not think it is fair to suppose that I thoroughly debauched my conscience, lost the sense of consistency, and thus paved the way for a career of dishonourable " Romanizing " in the Church of England. Subscription to the formulas of the party system is not an obligation of youth ; and if I chose my planks from either platform in turn, I do not think that I ever spoke seriously against my conscience.

On the other hand, I must have acquired an unenviable reputation for defending the indefensible. This, especially, at the meetings of smaller societies ; I have once, owing to a shortage of speakers, opened and opposed the same motion. But these were trivialities ; a far more serious consequence of this continual talking before audiences greedy of originality (I have talked at three separate meetings in one evening) is the extraordinary distaste for the obvious with which it indoctrinates the mind. You learn, in approaching any subject, to search at once for the point that is new, original, eccentric, not for the plain truth : you may be on the right side or the wrong, but you are constantly insisting on the side issues. Again and again I have had to ask myself whether I was not allowing this habit of mind to distort my ideas ; and to this day I am not certain that I should not have become a Catholic earlier if Catholicism were not so glaringly obvious. Apart, however, from this fear, which may be scrupulous, the debating habit is certainly a disqualification for public speaking, for you have to force yourself continually into the reflection that you are talking to simple people, and that what you think undeserving of mention, because commonplace, is to them a difficulty or an innovation.

I do not know whether the recalling of particular scenes, not directly connected with religion, is out of place in such a document as this, but to give some impression of one or two that force themselves on the memory may help the reader to gain an idea of what this club life was like. He must imagine me setting out, my dinner scarcely eaten, to a meeting of the Strafford, where Charles Marson, the priest-humorist of Hambridge (in Somerset) was reading a paper on " Toryism, Socialism, and the Catholic Church "—all allied movements, by his way of it, and certainly matter for some amazing epigrams. There was just time to drain my glass of port (no-heelers were the correct thing) in memory of King Charles and his faithful servant, and

then I must go on to the Fabian Society to hear a
Bishop's son pulverizing Nietzsche as an enemy of
democracy : and so back to Balliol, for a paper on
bird-life or some such subject at the " Decalogue "—
this is an actual evening.   He must picture Father
Bernard Vaughan in a crowded common-room at
Balliol thundering about the decadence of England,
and, after a pained speech in reply by a justly respected
fellow of the college, offering (to our almost audible
delight) to " shake hands with the gentleman who had
spoken for the middle classes." I wish I could convey
some idea of the Orthodox Club, that strange gathering
of nominal Socialists—Father Waggett, playing with
the tassels of his cassock-cord as he poured out delicate
paradoxes, Mr. Lindsay, of Balliol, picking his way
among them gingerly, " Joe " Legge, the clerical coach
of so many Trinity boats, standing to the full of his
enormous height, an Elizabethan figure, and recom-
mending the Class war as an excellent stimulus for
both parties concerned, while two puzzled members of
local Trade Unions sat wondering into what company
they had fallen, and Charles Lister nervously presided
behind the vermilion-painted balloting urns. And the
Canning, with its traditional mulled claret and long
churchwarden pipes, the latter (jealously affected by
myself) snapping in a disconcerting way whenever the
speaker reached his climax—here it was that I read
my paper about the Royal Commission on Ecclesiastical Discipline, the result of many weeks' browsing
among four blue-book volumes descriptive of Ritualistic services. The Union itself is less warm and com-

forting in retrospect, yet it leaves its indelible memories : Willie Gladstone rising for the tenth time to assure some frivolous interrupter that his question was out of order, with a pathetic dignity that belonged to earlier Parliaments : Mr. Belloc waggling a cigar between his fingers as he demolished the House of Lords : Mr. Winston Churchill pouring out fiery invective against Sir F. E. Smith, with whom he had travelled down in the train. Nor are these memories wholly political : I can see Mr. William Temple, still a layman and thought rather unorthodox, strumming softly on the piano in illustration of his paper on Browning—that was at the Shaftesbury : Father Stanton at the *De Rebus Ecclesiasticis*, before an audience of seventy in an undergraduate's room at St. John's, electrifying eager Ritualists with ten minutes of "pure Gospel," and then sitting on the edge of the table as he rolled out stories of the old days at St. Alban's, Holborn. If the object of undergraduate life be to gain experience of men and their ways of looking at things, assuredly I filled my measure ; but I am afraid little remains, apart from those grateful echoes which haunt and cheer the memory, except a complete inability to remain inattentive while a fellow-creature is on his legs, whatever his message, and a painful difficulty in restraining myself from taking the floor the moment he has sat down.

Meanwhile I was continuing my education. In my first summer I won the Hertford Scholarship, an award made on an examination in Latin only ; and my success here, as contrasted with the Ireland which

I did not get till my third year, made me think more
kindly of the Latin language, hitherto despised in
comparison with Greek. The love I afterwards acquired for the Latin tongue as something rich in
associations and lying at the roots (I think Mr. Belloc
says) of European culture, must have made it easier
for me to fall under the spell of the Latin Mass and the
Latin Office, as opposed to English translations and
adaptations of them. It is curious to reflect that of
the scholars of the immediate past only one was
familiar to me by name—his name was Martindale.

In the midst of these and other classical successes,
I only took a second in Mods ; an incident to which I
look back with regret, in so far as it must have been
caused by my own unnecessary immersion in other
ends, with satisfaction, because I do not suppose that,
but for this disappointment, I should have worked
properly for Greats, and with gratitude, because then
as in other times of failure I experienced such generous
sympathy from my friends.

" Greats " should, traditionally, involve the student
in doubts and searchings of heart about his religious
position : this does frequently happen, though more
(I am sorry to say) to the religious than to the unbelieving. I cannot remember meeting this experience
myself. At any time since I was seventeen I have had
" temptations against the faith," not so much against
particular articles in the creed as against the whole
system of religion : the existence of God and the sur-
vival of the soul after death have always been the
doctrines which, in this sense, presented difficulties

to me, though so many people seem to find it natural and easy to believe in them even (so far as that is thinkable) apart from the grace of faith. I sometimes wish I could get sixty people to sit down and write out a list of all the leading Christian doctrines in the order in which their unassisted intellect would find them probable. I believe the result would be both curious and reassuring; each of us would find that his stumbling-blocks, to several of his neighbours, were no stumbling-blocks at all. Anyhow, the only occasion I can recall on which an essay involved me in difficulties of conscience was when I had to write on free-will as opposed to determinism; and that was before I had started on Greats. I think that even before I left school I had come to think of the supernatural order as something to which Reason was not the key any more than Sense; that the Divine mysteries, capable as they are of being stated in reasonable terms, do not lie at the end of any chain of pure thought. The absolute of my philosophical authors was not, to me, the God whom I worshipped, loved, and feared; it was a neuter object, having no necessary existence in the real order of things, any more than those fine-spun abstractions with which the higher mathematicians amuse their emancipated brains. McTaggart was welcome to demolish Hegelian Theism; he was but throwing down Pelion from Ossa; Olympus remained unshaken.

But, while metaphysics affected me with this sense of unreality, the higher logic was, in my last year, meat and drink to me. It was the fashion to follow Dr. Bradley in his demolition of all previous logicians, and

then, in one's essays, to demolish Dr. Bradley himself.
Pragmatism was useful material for us puppies to tear
to pieces on the floor when we had finished with Mill
and the Sensationalists. Professor Cook-Wilson and
Professor J. A. Smith were the venerated heroes of our
campaigning. For myself, I early declared my intention of being "a crude realist" (my friend Patrick
Shaw-Stewart declaring himself a subjective idealist)
and lived up to my reputation fairly well.

I was, however, classic enough to go for inspiration
to the original Greek texts (a fortunate choice, I
believe, for the year in which I was examined). Plato,
with Dr. Caird to expound him, was alone worth all
the vapourings of the moderns. One of the best days
I have spent was that on which, in a space of nine
hours, I succeeded in reading the *Republic* from cover
to cover. Aristotle was a second favourite, from his
lack of literary appeal, but I suppose one learnt more
thought from him, if less dialectic.

As between Roman and Greek history (the other
chief subjects besides philosophy) my preference never
wavered ; the small compass of the documentary
evidence, with the consequent joy of inventing and
proving theories for yourself instead of accepting them
at second hand, prejudiced me altogether in favour of
the Greek. Nor, apart from a strong sympathy with
Cicero (another of my lost causes) did Roman history
ever stir my imagination, and admiration for the greatness of the Cæsars does not (apart from a few Virgilian references) form any part of the sentiment which
I feel towards the City of the Seven Hills.

A first in Greats left me neither a professional philosopher nor a professional historian ; but it left me with a fierce love of sifting evidence and the power of not being fascinated into acquiescence when superior persons talked philosophy at me.

V

BALLIOL—RELIGIOUS DEVELOPMENT

Defessi Aeneadae, quae proxima litora, cursu
Contendunt petere, et Libyae vertuntur ad oras.

AMID all this complication of atmosphere and fo
interests, in which I certainly lived very hard,
though with lamentably little to show for it, I was
observing, so far as obligations go, the life of a " prac-
tising Churchman." I never failed to " hear Mass "
on Sundays ; I can remember going to the Cowley
Fathers' church at six on a Sunday morning when
faced with an early motor-drive and a country-house
party all day. I abstained from meat on the appropriate days ; I ordinarily made my Communion every
Sunday, my Confession about four times a year. If I
give here some description of my three main religious
centres—Balliol Chapel, Pusey House, and the Cowley
Fathers' church—the external expression of my undergraduate religion will be sufficiently clear.

It would be silly for me to pretend that I ever loved
Balliol Chapel. As a building, it has defects almost
universally recognized. The tone of the ordinary
services was marked by a tradition of " superior "
music, indefinite dogma, and manly sentiment which
was vaguely supposed to propitiate the *manes* of the
late Dr. Jowett. Hymns with tricky little German

tunes, scraps of the Prayer Book selected under
Jowettian influence for daily repetition, books soiled
by the droppings of innumerable candles—I am afraid
it all made little appeal to me ; and though I kept
chapels rather than the substitute known as " rollers,"
it was only on Sunday at eight that the service meant
anything to me.   Two scholars besides myself were of
my own way of thinking ; the chaplain (the Rev. E. J.
Palmer, since Bishop of Bombay) was of that moderately Sacramental though not doctrinally rigid school
which has been common in Oxford since the publication of *Lux Mundi*.   There were few of us at those
early services, but there was a certain feeling of
brotherhood ; and the very fact of the empty seats
round you reminded you that you stood arrayed
against strong forces of moral indifference and spiritual
obscuration.   Outside of chapel, I saw much of Mr.
Palmer, and caught from him something of what I
shall describe later as being the dominant religious
tone of Oxford at the time.

But, to an undergraduate of my views, attendance
at a college chapel was dictated mostly by the sense
of duty : Pusey House was our spiritual home.   In
this establishment, which supports five priests with a
roving commission to look after undergraduates' souls,
and those more especially which derive their inspiration from the Oxford Movement, you found a spiritual
adviser always at hand, and a chapel always open for
devotion.   I was ear-marked as soon as I came up,
having met on my summer holiday in 1905 one of the
" Librarians " (in those days, you were not supposed

F

to know more than one of the librarians, for fear that their labours should overlap ; and though you had met them at meals, the other four would pass you on the staircase without even a monastic inclination of the head). He was, though not my Confessor, my director so far as I ever had one, and his advice as to my behaviour was, in every instance I can recall, both practical and edifying. When he retired, the then principal, the Rev. V. S. S. Coles, was to me, as to so many Oxford men of my generation, the natural person to apply to for help and for guidance.

Of the early morning celebrations in Pusey House Chapel I have the most grateful memories. To have dashed out of college through the chill mists of a November morning, to dive in suddenly from the street by a door that looked shut but was open, to mark on the stairs the wet footprints of fellow-devotees on bare oil-cloth, then suddenly to emerge from the neglected back-passage into carpeted floors and pictures and the comforts of habitation ; to hurry upstairs again, and so into the little green-panelled chapel, and worship there with the "few righteous men" of the University kneeling all round you—it conveyed a feeling, to me most gratifying, of catacombs, oubliettes, Jesuitry, and all the atmosphere of mystery that had fascinated me so long. I went, I suppose, on an average, about twice a week during my undergraduate time. It was here, too, that I learned to serve at the altar, though the position was something of a sinecure, since the usage of the chapel forbade all words and almost all ceremonies that were in excess of the minimum demanded by the Book of Common Prayer.

The Cowley Fathers' church I despair of describing to anyone who has not been, and indeed worshipped there. There is the Bodley Gothic; the Solesmes chant admirably rendered, so far as the inferior musical quality of the English words allows, by well-trained boys' voices; Father Waggett's preaching (if you were in luck that day), always stimulating and penetrating, sometimes provoking quite audible laughter; the solemn ceremonies, the reverent bearing of the ministers, and last, but above all, the friends you met there Sunday after Sunday and gossiped with on your way home—this was a whole separate world in the midst of your undergraduate world, an inspiration to look forward to, a memory to treasure. I pay this tribute all the more sincerely, because unwillingly. My love for Gothic was a calf-love which I was long in outgrowing; I find now no comfort but in the mellow splendour of the classical revival. The restrained Anglicanism which informed the ritual and ceremonies became to me later irritating in the extreme. What I have thought reverence I cannot but regard, in retrospect, as stiffness. But at the time Cowley was everything to me : the congregational hymns, ostentatious gestures, and profuse incense of St. Barnabas I condemned (Heaven help me l) as " Roman." To Cowley I would take my friends, of every and no denomination, in the hope of entrapping them into my own religion. And as the sacring-bell rang I would be seized by paroxysms of religious emotion, which I am afraid I valued more highly than (being chiefly nervous reaction) they deserved. I do not suppose that there were a dozen Sundays in all my undergraduate time when I did not attend St. John's Cowley at eleven.

It was to Cowley, too, that I went for my Confessions. I had, before I went to Oxford, asked my father's leave to do this ; he, though he was not in sympathy, of course, with the idea, had too much respect for my own conscience to put any obstacles in my way. He suggested my asking advice from Bishop Gore, then still at Birmingham, and it was Bishop Gore who recommended me to go to the late Fr. Maxwell, who afterwards became Superior. I looked upon him as my Confessor till his death in 1916, though owing to my absence from Oxford I never had occasion to tell him of the difficulties that were then troubling me. The atmosphere of the Cowley Mission-house was very different from the soft chairs, book-lined walls, and bright firesides of Pusey House. You found yourself isolated from all the world in a little bare room at the further end of the Community Chapel ; a grilled gate had closed behind you, and you had threaded your way down corridors that seemed depressingly clean. This sense of being quite shut off from the world lent to my confessions an awfulness which may well have been salutary, though Catholics would probably find it unpleasantly strange. Most converts, I suppose, find the Catholic Confessional more homely and off-hand than the Anglican. I used to go to Confession, I have said, four times a year at first, and probably not more than six times a year till after I came back to Oxford.

It will be seen from this account of my habits that I had by now " moved on " considerably since the time of my confirmation. It was not that I had felt, at any time, the religion in which I was brought up to be repulsive, or untrue, or even inadequate to my spiritual needs. I had not craved for light, or gone about advertising for religious innovations. I had accepted new views, reluctantly at first because they seemed too good to be true, but with no sense of revolution or going back on the past : they were an addition to, or rather a development of, my earlier teaching. Above all, they were not a second best which I chose in preference to Catholicism : I drifted into them. (I do not know if any of my readers notices the little Latin tags at the heads of these chapters, but that is what I meant by *quae proxima litora*—this was the first harbour which suggested itself.) At Balliol I was merely filling in with colour the outlines which had sketched themselves in my brain. During my first years there at least, and at the beginning of 1909, I was what from 1910 to 1915 I described, and I am afraid derided, as a " High Churchman."

For, with all these orthodoxies of practice, held together by some vague spirit of obedience to party regulations, I had no real doctrinal background for them. I genuflected and adored the Sacrament, yet my views about it were certainly not Catholic. I read Dr. Gore's book, *The Body of Christ*, and found it all but convincing, although in that earlier edition it was understood by many, and certainly by myself, as teaching no more than the " congregational " presence of Christ in the Mass—Christ present in the hearts of the faithful, the view commonly associated with the name of Hooker, and condemned as inadequate by Luther and the early reformers. The rival influence which prevented me from being quite satisfied was that of Father Waggett's book, *The Holy Eucharist*: Father Waggett was the hero of my school of thought, and it was to him or to his preaching I would introduce my friends, in the hope of impressing them. But certainly at this time I never thought of the Human Body of our Saviour, only of his Divine indwelling, as the secret of the Mass. And on this principle I would try to explain the Mass to myself in some way which should satisfy the Gospel language and the usage of the Church, yet dispense with the need of miracle.

This was not my only heterodoxy. I think I had lost my certainty about the direct effect of impetrative prayer. Certainly I was a Universalist, recoiling from the idea of hell ; and I remember an argument in which I assented to the possibility that souls after death were absorbed into a single Divine soul. Such speculations were not due to " difficulties " of my own, but to a desire to make the way easy and the walls surmountable to those who had no present belief in supernatural religion. This is, of course, the beginning of all Modernism ; you misinterpret the lack of faith in others as a need of intellectual conviction, and try to trim the sails of your theology accordingly. The ideas of Modernism I first heard explained by Mr. Rawlinson (afterwards of Christ Church) as we walked along the electric railway line between Blackpool and Rossall. A friend, who was with us, was properly shocked by the notion ; I did not defend it (nor did Mr. Rawlinson), but it seemed to me a tolerable attitude.

The Catholic Church had hardly crossed my path. I met Father Vaughan on the occasion when he spoke at the Union ; but I listened to him as to the representative of a strange religion. Father Benson I met once at tea in a friend's rooms ; he talked almost entirely about odd cases of nervous disease, and I was impressed by the originality of his conversation, but not by its charm. Nor did the Church even cross my path when, with two brothers, I paid a visit to Rome in the spring of 1907.

I was then, as I say, still in a fever of enthusiasm for the Gothic in architecture, the mediæval in church furniture and devotional atmosphere. Catholics, accustomed to worship at Downside or at the Oratory indifferently, will not easily realize the extent to which in the Church of England the mediævalist movement has been captured and exploited by a comparatively moderate party. Broadly speaking (of course there are exceptions), " Gothic " and " Renaissance " accessories symbolize a difference not of taste but of view ; the Gothic belongs to the " loyal " Churchman who takes his stand on the practice of the early Church, and fulminates continually against " Roman " innovations. " Gothic " accessories predominated at Cowley, and my pre-Raphaelitism approved it whole-heartedly. It is easy to imagine the effect of such tastes on one visiting Rome for the first time. I explored conscientiously the ruins of a dead past; I "did" the pictures; but (though it was Holy Week) I heard nothing at St. Peter's but a smattering of Tenebrae and part of High Mass on Easter Day, and I attended no other Catholic service except that of the Uniat rite on Holy Saturday at San Nicolo da Tolentino. Meanwhile, I worshipped most days at the Anglican Church of All Saints in the Via Babuino, whose very walls seem to cry out to the home-sick Anglican the motto, " *Ubi Mowbray, ibi Ecclesia.*"

Our *pension* was kept by Catholics; I used to admire the cassock of a Monsignore who sometimes dined there, and I remained proof against the arguments of a Presbyterian Dean, who, sitting at our table, reproached me with favouring the " eastward position " when the high altar at St. Peter's faced west. But, though most of our unbelieving fellow-lodgers easily did so, I never attended an " interview " with the Holy Father, nor did any of the pious usages of the Eternal City inspire me with feelings of anything but amusement. It was here I first met Mr. Urquhart, a fellow of Balliol and a Catholic; but even with this cicerone I learned no more than a chastened interest in early Mosaics.[1]

At the time of which I am speaking, I do not think it had come into my head to wonder what authority I had for worshipping as I worshipped. Of course I knew the case for Anglican orders, and was prepared

[1] The name of Rome has always, for me, stood out from any printed page merely because its initial is that of my own name. As early as I can remember, red was my favourite colour, and robins and roses (perhaps ordinary tastes) shared the preference.

to argue with anybody about "continuity"; but I cannot remember that I ever went further back than this. My actions were, as a matter of fact, dictated to me not by a Church but by a party; I was a party man, and known for a party man, and I had to live up to the rôle. It was a schoolboy, was it not, who, when asked if he could give a better instance of moral courage than a boy who said his prayers in a dormitory where twenty other boys didn't, replied on reflection that it would be still braver if a Bishop, put in a dormitory with twenty other Bishops, went to bed without saying any prayers at all. The same spirit of *noblesse oblige* attaches to the conduct of an undergraduate who is marked down as a "High Churchman"; externally, he meets with all encouragement from those of his own school, internally, he has a standard to live up to. Nor is that standard even a fixed one; for, confronted by some doctrine or practice more "advanced" than those he has hitherto countenanced, he feels it a kind of party treason to draw the line short of it. And as the British Empire (if its admirers are to be believed) was won in a fit of absence of mind, so our undergraduate finds that he has taken up the advanced man's burden, and even if it grows heavier he must (like the altruistic Imperialist) go through with it. He learns to defend his faith Biblically, traditionally, and rationally; it does not occur to him to wonder where the dictating voice comes from.

When I describe myself as a party man I must not be taken to mean that I lived entirely with one set of

people, never learnt to exchange views with or realize
the position of those who differed with me. Rather,
in our time, the Pusey House sort of undergraduate
spent most of his time in fraternizing either with
Evangelicals or with Nonconformists, to show that
there was no ill-feeling. If I describe the way in which
I spent the Long Vacation of 1908 I think it will serve
to illustrate the rather exacting claims my then position made upon me.

Towards the end of July I went to Baslow in Derby-
shire, where the Student Volunteer Movement held,
in Chatsworth Park, an annual Feast of Tabernacles
under the eye of heaven. The word " volunteer " is
to be understood here not in a military but in a missionary sense : we were a whole band of pious young
men from all over England and from various places
overseas. We slept in tents or in marquees (the
Oxford tent must have held quite fifty), we fed like a
Sunday school, we wore badges recording our names
and places of education ; we walked or bicycled far
and wide ; we met for prayer meetings under trees ;
we sat and listened to English dignitaries and Ameri-
can missionaries who gave us devotional addresses or
planned out for us (in a tone which to me seemed
almost Jingo) the evangelization of the world in this
generation. Persons of all creeds were admitted, so
long as they acknowledged Jesus Christ to be God—
a broad-mindedness of which the Tractarians would
probably have disapproved ; but in our day Mr. Coles,
after some preliminary doubts, had given it the Pusey
House blessing, and many of the dons who held sacra-

mentalist views (Mr. Palmer, for instance) were loud in praise of the institution.[1]

I think I must have a kink somewhere in my constitution, for, though other like-minded people seemed to enjoy themselves and to experience great spiritual help, for myself I was vastly uncomfortable. I am not referring to creature comforts, though I will not pretend that I enjoy the gipsy existence ; nor on the other hand did I feel the slightest qualms of conscience about my position as an Anglican in thus fraternizing with the sectaries ; after all, it was only we Anglicans who met for Communion in the parish church. But I hated the extempore prayers, I distrusted the devotional harangues, the language of the missionaries left me cold, and, if the truth must be told, I did not like the pious young men. So far from broadening my outlook, the place drove me more and more into the company of a few Oxford friends ; I found my best spiritual consolation in the plain-song Compline which the representatives of the Mirfield community sang every night, under a flickering lantern and half drowned by Welsh revivalist choruses from close by, in their separate tent.

That this attitude on my part was not the result of blind partizanship for the Tractarian cause, I feel convinced by the memory of the occupation I indulged in immediately afterwards—the mission which my father held (and holds) yearly on the beach at Blackpool. A handful of clergymen and a dozen or so of us

[1] I once attended a Conference at Cuddesdon at which Anglicans and Nonconformists met to discuss their differences about orders and sacraments, and I can remember taking a rigid Anglican view when it was my turn to contribute to the discussion.

undergraduates lived in the school buildings at Rossall
for a fortnight, and twice or three times every day went
into Blackpool to hold services at various points on
the sands. The message delivered at these services was,
of course, in the main delivered in the Evangelical
manner, for that was the tradition of most of the clergy
who took part : my father was naturally the animating
spirit of the whole, and the present Bishop of Peter-
borough (then a vicar in Manchester) was one of the
favourite speakers. But, if only in deference to the
preferences of several of the undergraduates, the life
at Rossall had almost the privileges of a retreat ; the
Communion was celebrated every morning ; there was
Sext at midday, and Compline before we went to bed.
Here, in spite of all differences of view, I felt among
friends from the first, and I cannot describe how impressive I found the mission services in this and the
two succeeding years. A mission on the sands looks
dreary and even ridiculous when you are out of ear-
shot, but join the crowd, take up the Bassarid's
thyrsus, and you are transformed. And I think even
an unsympathetic passer-by would have turned with
something else than scorn to watch eight hundred
people, of all sorts and ages, singing " Lead, Kindly
Light " as the August sun died away into a crimsoned
sea.

For a month or so after this I was engaged in
ordinary holiday pursuits and (I hope) working for
Greats. Then it was the turn of a " Missionary Cam-
paign " at Leeds. Some forty or fifty undergraduates
were being let loose over all the Anglican churches of

that admirably organized town, to inspire it, by means of services, addresses, and public meetings, with yet more interest in the work of foreign missions. It always happened in these cases that there were not enough "high" churches to go round among the undergraduates of my own school, and though I went once to St. Saviour's (the church Pusey built) my lot was cast chiefly with moderate vicars and respectable congregations. I fretted a good deal at the discretion of these "loyal Anglican" circles, but I was certainly impressed with their business efficiency and organization; few English towns would give you a better idea of Anglicanism as a going concern. For the dissemination of Anglicanism I pleaded with all the spiritual fervour and all the flippant rhetoric I could command : I still blush at some of the oratorical vulgarities I was guilty of. Leeds has a long tradition, I was then aware, of clerical "losses" to the Catholic Church, but the record did not move me one way or the other ; my business was with Anglicanism as I saw it and Anglicanism as I wanted it to be—these huge and well-equipped churches filled with the scent of incense and offering to the world with every circumstance of spectacular adornment the drama of the Divine mysteries.

So much for the summer of 1908 ; it was the high-water mark of my undergraduate ecclesiastical activities, and it was the end, I think, of the period during which I was wholly satisfied with that type of Anglicanism which combines elaborate ritual and sacramental doctrine with what is known as "loyalty to the Prayer Book."

What, then, were the influences which led me—I recognize it now—to pass beyond the limits of the sober, albeit partisan, churchmanship which takes its stand upon the proved practice of the very early centuries, the unrepealed rubric of the Sixth Edward which orders the chancels to remain " as they were in time past," and the hesitating patronage extended to it by a sorely harassed episcopate ? Where did I first learn—if I may define the essence of things by their externals—to invoke the saints as a matter of course, to use the rosary, to adore the Sacrament in the Tabernacle, to acquiesce in the glorification of the Prayer Book Liturgy by additions from elsewhere, to treasure details of worship because Rome practised them, to find my authority in the traditions of Western Christendom and the pre-Reformation beliefs of the English Church ? It must have been a complex of influences, but it should be possible to disentangle some of the threads.

In the first place, I was beginning to see more of my religion up and down the country. I followed, *dum fortuna fuit*, the cult of the bicycle, not then stigmatized by the ignoble prefix of " push " ; and it was my custom to scrutinize every church (not forgetting the vestry and the notice-board) which stood open on my route. I schemed so as to arrange my halting-places (I thought nothing of eighty miles in a day) at towns where I should find in the morning a service suited to my own tastes. (I can still remember my disgust when, in the summer of 1907, I attended a church where " The Lord be with you " was frequently inserted, and the congregation did not join—as I did lustily—in the recitation of the Creed.) The result of these visitations was not to puzzle me with the varieties of Anglican usage ; I gloried in these, for I discerned everywhere an " upward " tendency ; but I think I was conscious everywhere of an atmosphere of artificial restraint ; always, even in the most favoured shrines, some detail of ornament or turn of phrase on a notice-board suggested the cozening of a jealous Bishop or the humouring of an unruly churchwarden. Why could they not (like myself on a straight stretch of down-hill road) " let it rip," and run the risk of concealed turnings without these jarring applications of the brake ? I cannot remember that I ever consciously formulated such thoughts, but I suspect that they must have been at work in me.

There was another more palpable influence—it must have been in 1909 that I first visited the community at Caldey, on a reading-party with several friends. *Notissima fama insula ;* fortunately it is not necessary for me to describe to Catholics the attractions of the island cloister ; there is a guest-house, and they can try it for themselves. I am afraid they will not find much that is externally altered since the community's Anglican days. But on my first visit the present chapel was not built, and four cells knocked together served instead. From the precarious gallery you felt at once extraordinarily close to the worship of the community, and extraordinarily apart from the cloistered sanctities of its life. In the guest-house, all the gossip of the church was told and retold : Bobby

Palmer, who once visited it with me afterwards, said that a stranger listening to the conversation might have imagined " bishops " to be the name applied to some secret band of criminals. It was at Caldey that I met priests who " said their Mass " every day ; that I regained and for the first time assimilated the doctrine of the intercession of saints ; that I became enamoured of the solemn cadences, the mysterious silences, the ever-varied monotonies of the Divide Office. It was at this time that I was given an office-book, one of the various English adaptations of the Breviary : I forget its real name ; Mr. Rawlinson (whom I have mentioned already) called it " the Book of Uncommon Prayer." During the latter part of my time at Oxford I said the day-hours pretty regularly, and the hypothesis that I was " saying quint " was invariably adopted by the friends who were in digs with me when I did not appear in time for meals. The use of Latin for devotional purposes had at the same time impressed me, and I used to make up little prayers and rhymed litanies of my own addressed to my favourite saints : one of them, I cannot be sure for what reason, was St. Hilary of Poitiers.

There were plenty of other considerations which Caldey ought to have suggested to me. Here was the Latin Mass, the Latin Office ; here were endless devotions of which any Anglican bishop must have disapproved—all continued not merely without the connivance, but without even the silence of an ecclesiastical superior ; there was, outside the community, no ecclesiastical superior. I do not say this with any

desire to criticize Caldey ; for there is, after all, no legal
regulation in the Anglican Communion which con-
templates the existence of religious orders, and consequently there is no machinery for their control ;
while the Caldey monks were on diocesan soil, they
were in direct relations with the Bishop of the diocese ;
when they came to live on an extra-diocesan island, it
was hard to know what they were to do. Of course,
on any strict theory of jurisdiction, the hearing of
Confessions on the island was a highly dubitable practice ; but then Anglicans everywhere are shy of strict
theories of jurisdiction. The effect of Caldey on me
was to let me see, in microcosm, a vision of a revived
pre-Reformation church, and on returning to the
mainland I must have tended to measure the satis-
factoriness of the churches I visited by the degree in
which they approximated to the island ideal. This
was especially true of the Reservation of the Blessed
Sacrament, then far less common than it is now (I
doubt if there were more than a dozen London churches
at the outside which practised it : only half a dozen
were generally known to do so, and these in circumstances discouraging adoration). The value of devotions to the Blessed Sacrament was now a clear article
of my creed, and was to become the chief cause for
which I was prepared to do battle.

Yet I can remember points on which I was still at
variance with Catholic notions. Thus I wrote to one
friend (Ted Shuttleworth) to explain that I did not
personally believe in the Immaculate Conception, and
regarded the Assumption as impossible ; I used to

rally another friend (Maurice Hugessen, who afterwards became a Catholic, and was killed at the Somme)
on the use of the rosary. This was in the summer of
1909 ; in the summer of 1910 I was using a rosary
myself ; and when I went to Mirfield I remember
being told that I was the first person who had said his
beads in their chapel since Hugh Benson left them.
But it is to the summer of 1909 that I trace my first
real consciousness of the unique position of the Mother
of God ; it was a sermon preached by Mr. Child at St.
James's, Plymouth, that first roused me to speculation
about it.

During my last visit at Oxford I succeeded in cur-
tailing to some extent my visiting-list and my engage-
ment-book, as became one living in digs and working
under the immediate imminence of Greats. But, to
keep in touch with friends who to some extent held my
own views, I used to be at home every Friday to a
select circle—the occasion was known as "Catholic
Tea." Numbers varied from two or three to ten or
eleven, but during the whole time of its continuance,
down to Easter, 1915, I can only remember one Friday
on which nobody came.

But, at the same time, I was more and more coming
into contact, outside Oxford, with people who very
definitely shared my views, and to some extent
modelled them ; people who definitely belonged to the
Maximalist wing of the Oxford Movement, laid great
stress on "Latin," as opposed to mediæval, accessories
of worship, disavowed the tacit truce which had come
to exist between us and the Bishops since the latest

ritual prosecutions, insisted that modern "Roman" devotions were the only means of touching the hearts of an indifferent nation, assigned willingly to Peter the primacy of the Church, and only differed as to how much more was due to him. This last consideration was one which had never troubled me before ; I do not think that it actually troubled me now ; but unconsciously the Papacy came to take a place, wholly undefined and calling urgently for consideration, in the horizon of my mind. I suppose I allowed it to be assumed that I was a Papalist without troubling to scrutinize my own theory of the Church ; this process came later.

The word "a Romanizer" should be capable of being used in two senses. Μηδίζειν in Greek means "to adopt a policy of *rapprochement* with the Medes " (a harsher translation might be found) ; σκυθίζειν means "to imitate the manners of the Scythians." In this latter sense I became consciously a Romanizer at the time of my leaving Oxford ; in the former sense I might have accepted the description out of bravado, but had not yet, intellectually, tied myself down to a formula. Perhaps the two tendencies unconsciously react upon one another. But the admiration for things Roman, as opposed to Rome itself, was for the first time definitely impressed on my mind upon the occasion of a visit to Belgium, just after taking Greats.

I had been with a friend (Mr. Samuel Gurney) to Munich and Ober-Ammergau for the Passion play ; we came back by way of Belgium, and joined there another friend (the Reverend Maurice Child) and three others who were like-minded. Belgium was not yet glorified with the halo of martyrdom ; we wandered about Dinant Cathedral, and drank chocolate at a restaurant that looked out on the Cloth Hall of Ypres. But the extraordinary devotion of the people wherever we went, and especially at Bruges, struck home with a sense of immeasurable contrast to the churches of one's own country, half-filled on Sundays, shadowily peopled on week-days by a faithful few. Bruges itself we declared to be the Holy City : the tourist, I know, thinks of it as *Bruges la morte*, but then the tourist does not get up for early Masses—he would find life then. Or, if the effort be too much for him, he can at least go on Friday morning to the chapel of the Saint Sang and witness the continuous stream of people that flows by, hour after hour, to salute the relic and to make their devotions in its presence ; he would find it hard to keep himself from saying, like Browning at High Mass, " This is too good not to be true." There was much in Belgium which could not be transplanted to England, but could not Benediction, free access to the Tabernacle, the teaching of frequent Communion, and admission to Communion for children, with all the brightness and gaiety, the businesslike movements and the casual homeliness of the churches, be reproduced in the Church of England in time to save our country from lapsing into heathenism ?

Just before I went in for Greats, I received through my brother (who had been at Trinity) a suggestion which was to determine my outward circumstances for many years. Partly through him, and partly

through my Eton friends, I already enjoyed the friendship of that venerable figure in Trinity Common-room,
Mr. R. W. Raper. Mr. Lloyd, then chaplain of the
college, was to leave in two years' time ; and a fellowship then vacant was naturally ear-marked for a future
chaplain. The suggestion that I should allow myself
to be proposed took me completely by surprise : I
had once told a friend that I would never accept a
position which involved teaching Honour Moderations,
or serving a church which did not have High Mass on
Sunday—this offer, it appeared, contradicted both
resolutions. But I had no immediate ideas for the
future ; my mind was harassed by impending examinations, and the friends whom I consulted thought it
would be right for me to allow my name to be considered. If, from Trinity's point of view, the arrangement was an unhappy one, I can plead that I drifted
into acceptance without taking all future possibilities
into account ; for myself, I can never cease to bless
whatever mixture it was of inertia and self-pleasing
that led me to accept ; I found a new home, and
friendships such as are not easily gained in a lifetime.
In a Senior Common-room (*experto crede*) a new fellow
is not elected in a day, and I think it must have been
at the Hotel Harscamp at Namur (do the waiters still
remember, in spite of the German occupation, a certain
farmyard imitation of a diocesan conference ?) that I
decided to write to the President in acceptance of a
teaching fellowship with expectation of a chaplaincy.

VI

TRINITY AND ORDINATION

Ergo avidus muros inceptae molior urbis
Pergameamque voco, et laetam cognomine gentem
Hortor amare focos, arcemque attollere tectis.

IT was in this summer of my leaving Balliol (1910)
that I first attended a Catholic service in England.
It was the Feast of the Assumption, and the devotional book I used (*Catholic Prayers*, compiled under
the direction of the Rev. A. H. Stanton) gave me to
understand that it was a feast of obligation : the
Anglican church at Lyme Regis, where I was then
staying with my family, had no celebration that day
and I slipped across the valley to the little Catholic
chapel to fulfil my obligation. I never became a
haunter of Catholic churches ; indeed, till I went to
Farnborough, I doubt if I had worshipped with Catholics in England as many as a dozen times : St. Aloy-
sius', Oxford, I have never entered to this day. I
never had any theoretical disapproval of the practice,
but I did not see any point in playing about with it.

I was to have a term's leave of absence before taking
up my residence at Trinity, and it was during this
time that an incident happened which was of considerable importance in my life. It is not a guilty
conscience, but respect for the feelings of others, that

forbids me to specify the circumstances in detail : in outline they were as follows—I undertook a tutorial appointment for that autumn, which was in no sense of a religious nature ; but, coming to realize that the person under my charge was in need of spiritual assistance, I could not do otherwise than endeavour to give it. Those who had employed my services objected, when they found that this was happening, on the ground that they disapproved of my views, and the choice was offered to me of continuing my work on the understanding that I would be silent on religious subjects, or of throwing up the appointment. I would have preferred from the point of view of my own feelings to do the former ; but consultation with my Confessor assured me that it would be an impossible strain upon my conscience to acquiesce in the condition laid down. I therefore left, not without some sense of ill-usage at the time (for I was not accustomed to think of myself, then, as an ecclesiastical outlaw), but, I hope, without giving any needless trouble. There was no room for me at Trinity, and by the kindness of the Principal (Dr. Darwell Stone) I was allowed to live at Pusey House for the latter part of that Michaelmas term.

This was the only period—a period of about a month and a half—when I ever experienced before 1915 an attack of what Anglicans call "Roman fever." On the very threshold of my career it was suddenly brought home to me that my view of Anglicanism was not one of the numerous theories of it which are tolerated in respectable circles ; indeed, it was hinted to me at the time (I have since thought, only rhetorically) that

I would have done better to be an out-and-out Roman Catholic. It seemed as if my vision was to be rudely dispelled. I had held that the English people were irremediably prejudiced against Rome ; therefore, if they were to learn anything of the grace of Communion, of Sacramental Confession, of the Communion of the Saints, and so on, it must be a party within the Church of England which should instruct them. The Roman Catholics (as I once put it) have to serenade the British public from the drive : we Anglican Catholics have the entrée to the drawing-room. Well, I had tried on Anglican Catholicism in the drawing-room, and found that it meant the door-mat. Could Anglicanism be justified when it did not even succeed ?

I must have thought then, vaguely and half-consciously, of submission to Rome. I should have been wrong—I mean, I should have been doing the right thing from the wrong motives. I should have been influenced by agitation, by petulance, by anything rather than the inspiration of the Holy Ghost. The " Brighton troubles " had just happened ; and, as is usual in such times of crisis, any Ritualist who was down on his luck and out of work looked upon Rome as a sort of Waifs and Strays Home for persons in his situation. The conception, it need hardly be said, is flattering to neither communion ; and the man who yields to such transitory feelings may very well become a nuisance to his new church as to the old—*Trojae et patriae communis Erinnys*. I should have saved myself years of misery, but I should have come with a wrong intention. As it was, the friendly sympathy of the Rev. Walter

Carey, then one of the Pusey House librarians, did much to restore my courage and prepare me for new effort.

At Trinity, whatever misgivings they may have had about my ecclesiastical future, my colleagues made room for me without any hint of suspicion or disapproval. It would not be becoming in me to praise the living, but there were two to whose memories I cannot but pay tribute here—Mr. Raper, who, strongly as he disagreed with my point of view, never ceased to take an interest even in my ecclesiastical career, and Mr. Tiddy, whose sparkling gift for friendship gave me so much solace in perhaps the loneliest time of my life. For I was lonely ; my old friends had mostly gone down, and the undergraduates of the time did not quite know what to make of this peculiar foundling which Balliol had left at their gates. With the new year which began in autumn, 1911, I had no such difficulties : they found me already ordained and in full work, and treated me as an institution of the place ; and when I began to be at home on Wednesday evenings with coffee and port and barrow-loads of bananas, even official restraints slipped away, and I felt an undergraduate once more. But in the two first terms of 1911 I was little in touch with college life and gravitated, if only for company's sake, to the society of dons, and principally, of course, clerical dons.

Of these there were two special groups, predominantly clerical, whom I met every week. On Mondays the Monday lunch (or munch, for short) introduced me to a set of young clerical fellows, differing widely in orthodoxy but all of Sacramental tradition, who gossiped and intrigued about university politics over (it must be confessed) a well-spread table. The "Friday lunch" was at once more ascetic and less homogeneous. On the one side, we said Sext before luncheon and None afterwards (rather to the confusion of unwary scouts' boys, who would bring in the fish-slice at the wrong moment) ; we ate, naturally, no meat, and milk puddings only were the orthodox sequel. On the other side, the party was not wholly clerical ; its conversation had a certain modernist smack about it ; and its *personnel* covered, nominally at any rate, a wider range of churchmanship. On Monday you would hear Mr. Ollard of St. Edmund's Hall and Mr. Williams of Exeter holding very candid language about some latitudinarian dignitary, for whom, at best, Mr. Thompson of Magdalen would be putting up a half-hearted defence ; on Friday, Mr. Talbot of Balliol and Mr. Rawlinson of Christ Church would be wrangling over the latest German heresy, with Mr. Brook of Merton labouring to keep the peace. "There is no place like Oxford for gossip" Bishop Gore once warned me, and certainly after a few ex-periences of these rival symposia one had little respect left for grey hairs or for scarlet hoods, and the thoughts of many clerical hearts were revealed.

My closest ally in arms at this time was a member of the Monday institution—the Rev. N. P. Williams, of Exeter. To both of us, in details of ritual and of devotional practice, "East—West : Rome's best" might have served for a motto. "Knaves and fools

we both despised alike "—ecclesiastical authorities
whose policy seemed so to sin against the light that it
had to be put down to folly, and thinkers whose views
were so intolerably vague that it seemed only charitable to attribute them to knavery. We had friends in
common, too, outside the university, and to some
extent haunted the same congenial churches during
our vacations. On one point, however, we were and
have remained hopelessly at issue. To him, the word
"Catholic" connoted the threefold hierarchy, a
nominal adhesion to the Nicene Creed, and a permanent
possibility of seven Sacraments ; whatever body
passed these tests, whether it were Roman, Eastern,
Anglican, or "Old Catholic," was part of the Church :
the Pope was conceded a grudging primacy of honour
only, not of jurisdiction. To me (as I shall try to make
clear in the next chapter) there were only two sets of
people who mattered—Roman Catholics and Anglicans ; and to justify the fact of the distinction while
reducing the distinguishing features to a minimum
was my constant study. Further, as a trained theologian, he had a certain jealousy in the abstract for a
chastened liberty of speculation ; I had no interest in
discovering the truth, but (believing myself to have
found it) in making people believe it. "But you must
give *some* explanation of the Reformation," I remember his saying as we walked past the palings of St.
John's Cowley one afternoon, and I replied excitedly,
"Just like sin." We seldom broke off these arguments
without my telling him that he was a Protestant, and
his telling me that I lived in an unreal world and ought

to be a Papist ; yet the next moment we would be planning some common scheme, or enjoying some joke which needed community of theological thought to make it amusing.

As for my ecclesiastical circle outside Oxford (chiefly consisting of unbeneficed clergymen), it would be easy to represent us as a set of unruly young men, bigoted about doctrines and frivolous about persons. Neither accusation, in retrospect, strikes me as wholly true. The fact is, on the one side, that we all believed in (Roman) Catholicism as a system which worked, which held the ordinary man and attracted the poor where Anglicanism did not ; we all agreed that the Roman system—the preaching of Penance and attendance at Mass as obligatory, the preference for short and businesslike services, the attempt to stimulate devotion by means of the rosary, benediction, etc.—was the right way of going about things : our only difference between ourselves was how much of it could be done prudently, and how much of it an intelligent theory of Anglicanism would carry. Hence, from the very nature of our ideals, we were out of sympathy with those who took Anglicanism as a working basis and vaguely tried to " brighten " it. On the other hand, having a university education, the confidence of youth, and a pressed-down measure of the gift of humour, we declared eternal war on cant, on Proudieism with its parasite Thumbledom, on clergymen who pulled long faces, talked in unnatural voices, breathed an atmosphere of artificial heartiness, or, in general, behaved in a fashion for which I coined the epithet "unctimonious." A certain sort of

" clerical voice " with the invariable address, " dear brother," was current coin among us. " Six young unmarried clergymen, born before their time, are looking out for a loyal, tractable vicar "—this was how some of my friends began an advertisement designed for the *Church Times ;* and perhaps it is not surprising that the *Church Times* never put it in.

Into this brotherhood I came as a junior; my friends were mostly ordained before me. But I do not think I can be accused of going about my candidature for ordination in a light or irresponsible spirit. Certainly, so far as the examinations went, I took myself seriously. The papers set to ordination candidates in the Church of England have been the subject of much legitimate criticism; no one has done this more pungently than Charles Marson in his exquisite brochure *And Ard.* The most zealous defenders of Anglicanism can scarcely maintain that " Where was Nob ? " is a very fruitful question to put to the accomplished seminarist. The fact is, I suspect, that these examination papers are meant simply for a test, at once of decent intellectual faculties and of comparative doctrinal orthodoxy : it is not even hoped by those in authority that the Anglican deacon, or even the Anglican priest, will really have " learnt his job " before ordination. At theological colleges some sound practical and some good critical theology is taught, and in certain cases learnt, but the Bishop's examination is no test of these.

For myself, I thought I had better follow the vagaries of the higher criticism before my diaconate, leaving

moral theology (in which I was determined to have
some grounding) to my preparation for the priesthood.
Taking advice from a friend (the Rev. R. G. Parsons,
then fellow of Univ.), I read Buddhe on the Religion
of Israel, Preservéd Smith (familiarly known as
" Damned Smith " to theologians) on Old Testament
History, Scott on the Fourth Gospel, and above all
Schweitzer's *Quest of the Historical Jesus*, which
was then the last word with the liberal school. All
these I faithfully plastered with annotations at the
side, conceived in a very ill-tempered tone, for the
books annoyed me. I also underlined the whole
of the first three Gospels in the original Greek with
different coloured chalks, to see which passages were
common to all three, which to two, which were
unique.

I shall have to return to the question of these critical
studies in the next chapter but one, in connexion with
the subject of authority. Here it remains for me to
give some idea of my doctrinal course, which I took in
a more practical but, I hope, not in a less conscientious
spirit. To me, and I suppose to many people, the
paper on the Thirty-nine Articles is a test not so much
of intellect or of industry as of theological disposition.
The articles stretch before you like a row of hurdles
in an evil dream, and somehow or another you are
bundled over each in turn. There are various inter-
preters eager to give you a shove from behind; the
most potent of these is Santa Clara, the Catholic priest
of *John Inglesant*. His work, proving that the
Anglican articles are wholly in accord with Trent, has

no doubt been forgotten by Catholics, but I believe some Anglicans invoke its aid before Ordination. Then there is Bishop Forbes of Brechin, a sturdy Anglo-Catholic : I never saw either of these books. My own needs were served by the present Bishop of Glouces-ter's manual ; it was officially recommended, and I took it to be a purely dispassionate exegesis ; but I have since thought it was written with the idea of making things smooth for the Sacramentalist. It insists, for example, that the Articles can only be under-stood as condemning the Council of Trent where it is certain that that particular clause was posterior in date to the corresponding clause in the Tridentine definitions. But even so, I had to make some im-provements of my own upon Dr. Gibson before I felt happy.

There are two obvious ways of reconciling oneself to the Articles—and, when I use that phrase, let me state clearly that I believe only a handful of Anglican clergy-men could really subscribe to the whole document *au pied de la lettre*. How many Anglicans really believe that " good works done before the grace of Christ . . . have the nature of sin ? " (This was, in fact, the article which troubled me most of all, striking as it did at my favourite scholastic doctrine of congruous merit.) But I digress. In reconciling yourself to this formula, you may take a narrowly legalistic view, and, examin-ing every phrase in barrister's fashion according to the strict letter, find a loophole of escape by means of faulty wording. Thus I think it is contended that the " Romish " doctrine of Purgatory, relics, etc., can be distinguished from the " Roman " doctrine—the contemptuous word implies that the reference is only to abuses—and so on. Or you can take precisely the opposite point of view, and say, " After all, this is only a rough and ready formula. Everybody accepts it, but nobody worries about it in detail. As long as you can give it a general assent you are all right." Both these methods are open ; I think, now, that I made the mistake of combining the two, adopting now an ultra-literalist view, now a merely common-sense view ; and of course you cannot really have it both ways. I was not properly an Anglican either according to the letter or according to the spirit.

Do I reproach myself ? I am not quite sure that I do. I was (and am) perfectly certain that my subscription was no less conscientious (to put it at the lowest) than that of many liberal Churchmen,[1] many of whom have been rewarded with dignities and canonries. *De facto*, it seems to me, the walls of the Church of England have been broken down ; unless and until the authorities take steps to build them up all round, I do not see that they can complain if the Sacramentalist avails himself of the breaches which the Socinian has made for him. As things are at present, I do not see how a man can be too " advanced " for the Church of England unless he feels bound to make his submission to the Church of Rome.

This was not my thought at the time. Here and

---

[1] Nothing is more clearly stated in the articles, few things are less generally believed among Anglican theologians, than the corporal Ascension.

there Dr. Gibson helped me ; how I could help Dr. Gibson presented little difficulty. He held, if I remember right, that the Church of England allowed the belief in probation, but not in actual purgation, after death. What was the value of such a distinction ? How could a soul be " proved " except by circumstances of toil or pain, and how could toil or pain do other than purify ? By making (as it seemed to me) a few logical deductions from his own premises, I found myself clear of doubt. Remember that I was not choosing between the Church of England and the Church of Rome ; my heart was all in the Church of England, not as a system of dead formulas, but as a living body of people to whom I had a message (though my voice were but an inconsiderable cry) to return to the old paths and renew the waste places ; I wanted, with all my soul, to enter the Anglican ministry. And if I could by any means persuade myself that my interpretation was tolerated, I could not hesitate to go forward.

Not that I would conceal anything or have any reservations, as far as I could avoid it. It was for this reason, I hope, rather than from any desire to "draw" my examiners, that in referring to the article " of Christ alone without sin " I definitely asserted the Immaculate Conception. One of the chaplains wrote to me and asked if I asserted this as a matter of faith : I answered No, that I asserted it as a general belief, like the belief that the Fourth Gospel was written by St. John. My own conscience demanded no more than this, and on the eve of my Ordination the Bishop of Reading re-

H

peated to me " Pious belief ? Yes. Defined doctrine ?
No."[1]

Certainly the period before my diaconate was not an
untroubled one. There was much talk at the time of
the Prayer Book being reformed by the Convocations :
some concessions were to be made to us, certain others
to the Broad Churchmen, and we were all to live
happily ever after. It is melancholy to reflect that
these proceedings are still dragging on in 1917, with
most unexpected results. One of the concessions to us
was to be the renewed observance of King Charles's
Day : this was agreed to just in time to be pounced
upon by the *Westminster Gazette* as a bolstering up of
Tsarism ! The Broad Churchmen were to be made
happy, above all, by the excision of those passages in
the Psalms in which King David curses his enemies,
together with their widows and orphans, in the language of justifiable irritation. This, too, was passed,
but it was passed in the air-raid season, and the *Daily
Express* came out with the whole-page headline,
" BISHOPS BOYCOTT DAVID'S REPRISAL PSALMS." *Heu
vatum ignarae mentes !* At the time, these issues were
not foreseen, and it was only the Tractarian wing of
the Church itself which took alarm at the modernizing
tendencies. I went to a meeting about it at Margaret
Street, where crises in the Church are invested with a
peculiar atmosphere of delicious trepidation ; I wrote
an article in the *English Church Review* demurring to

---

[1] At the time of my ordination I took a private vow, which I always
kept, never to preach without making some reference to our Lady, by
way of satisfaction for the neglect of other preachers.

the proposal of a " permissive use " of the Eucharistic vestments.

Nor was I myself free from alarms. A certain devotional sodality called " The League of our Lady " was setting up a " chapter " in Oxford, and in a moment of inertia I consented to accept some sort of presidential position on the strict understanding that it was to involve no activity on my part. The result was that my name appeared, with no sanction from myself, at the foot of a printed notice inviting the members to a preliminary meeting. The secretary who Englished it has long since become a Catholic, and I do not think he will mind my saying that the wording of it was a bit " sticky." I will not ask what friendly hand it was that forwarded this notice to Dr. Paget, then Bishop of Oxford ; anyhow, I was summoned to the Diocesan Registry and interrogated about the phrase " clients of Mary." I suggested that if you had a patron saint you were, by mere force of language, a client of that saint ; the Bishop did not seem much impressed by the argument. But, having understood that my position was that of a sleeping partner, he let me off with a caution.

Among other kind concessions he had agreed that, as a proper course of studies was impossible in view of my residence at Trinity, I might spend the summer months in retreat at Caldey in lieu of a theological college. To Caldey accordingly I went, to live in the monastery this time (I had already paid three visits to the island) and to do my own reading there. I was greeted on my arrival by the news that the Father

Abbot was away, attending a Conference on the Prayer
Book Reform crisis at Lord Halifax's house at Hickleton. It was intimated to me, further, by Fr. Gately
(now a Catholic priest at St. Catherine's, Birmingham, then a Caldey novice) that the crisis had caused
grave searchings of heart among the community,
and that if the Father returned unsatisfied, it would
probably mean the immediate submission of the community to Rome. My position as a candidate for the
diaconate seemed likely to be precarious, but I waited
in hope. A strong resolution was passed at Hickleton,
a commemorative tree planted, and Abbot Aelred
returned in peace.

This was not the end of excitements. It was the
summer of 1911 ; the railway strike broke out, and
for a short time Tenby was cut off from all communi-
cations with the east ; Mr. Pomeroy, the steward of
the island, only reached it by boat in order to be
present on the Feast of the Assumption. And one
night, while all this was going on, the Abbot told us
before Compline that, according to a mainland rumour,
Germany had just declared war on England. It was
not (it will be remembered) far from the truth, but
this storm also blew over. And in spite of all storms,
I passed at Caldey seven weeks of extraordinary
happiness and peace. Thinning out carrots in the
gardens with a fierce sun beating on my cassock, bathing with the community in recreation on those interminable days of sunshine, standing in a blaze of light
at Vespers, or in almost complete darkness at Compline, while the slow cadences of the Divine Office

rolled over my head, hurrying out to Matins before break of dawn along a razor's edge path past the quarry garden—I do not think that, whatever its effect on my divinity, a theological college could have provided me with more of religious inspiration for my coming ministry.

Coincidences do happen, and I confess my journey back should have put thoughts into my head. At Tenby Station I met a Cambridge acquaintance, one of the few Catholic friends I then had, and travelled with him part of the way. When I had left him, a stranger in the carriage asked to see my breviary, and conversation revealed the fact that he was a Catholic and an old Trinity man. Fate seemed to be laughing at my Anglican ambitions. And then the discovery that the President of Trinity was also travelling in the same train reminded me that I had put my hand to the plough.

Bishop Paget had died that summer, and the Bishop of Reading took the Ordination. The retreat was held at Keble, the Ordination at the Cathedral. One of my most vivid memories is the Bishop's last talk to me before the ceremony about the duty of constantly asking for guidance from the Holy Spirit—a duty sadly neglected, I am afraid, until times of trouble forced me back upon it in circumstances other than he or I then contemplated. I had no scruples of conscience or prickings of doubt as I knelt to receive the rite, and it was with a feeling of unmixed elation that I travelled back to Manchester, *voti compos*, ordained to the diaconate.

VII

ENFANT TERRIBLE

Tu nunc Karthaginis altae
Fundamenta locas, pulchramque uxorius urbem
Exstruis, heu regni rerumque oblite tuarum.

FROM the time of my Ordination up to the time
of my reception, a space of six years, I read the
full office of the Latin breviary daily, excusing myself
only in circumstances (such as ill-health) where a
Catholic priest would be excused. Nor did I regard
this as merely a private preference, though few of my
friends did the same ; it was not that vocal prayer
particularly appealed to me, though the sense of
praying the daily prayer of the whole Church cannot
be without its inspiration. I did it from the first with
a feeling of obligation, and should have regarded it as
(for me) a mortal sin to do otherwise, just as I should
have regarded it as (for me) a mortal sin to contract
matrimony. Catholics will think this peculiar : I am
reserving the explanation of my ideas about authority
till the next chapter. Here I will only say that I
regarded the Church of England as a section of the
Latin Church, and, having been ordained to minister
in a section of the Latin Church, did not think it right
to excuse myself from the obligations of the Latin clergy
just because desuetude and the concessions made by

secular authorities at the Reformation had encouraged my clerical brethren to do so. At the same time, my Confessor insisted that, by a rubric of the Prayer Book, I was bound to read Morning and Evening Prayer according to the Anglican rite—this takes anything from a quarter of an hour to twenty-five minutes a day. I accepted this at his direction (I discontinued the practice after his death in 1916), regarding it as a sort of penance for the schismatical acts of my forefathers. I admit that the double obligation sometimes necessitated the recitation of " my office " at odd moments, but it was an exaggeration when a friend of mine, asked how I was, replied, " Oh, just as usual ; a week ahead with the Breviary, and a week behind with the Prayer Book." Actually I kept the rules.

Another clericalism I adopted was the custom of wearing a cassock—indoors as a matter of course, and even out of doors when I was within the college buildings, or was on my way through the streets to undertake any clerical duty. In this I did not differ from many of my friends, but what passes without remark in a parish is liable to excite comment in a university. My argument was that since I belonged to the Church of the country there was no reason for me to sneak about in trousers like a recusant priest, and I believed that the system ought to be encouraged : that if a few more people familiarized the public with the cassock as ordinary clerical dress, it might become as natural in England as it was in the country of my dreams, Belgium.

My clerical duties in college were very slight ; Mr.

Lloyd, the chaplain, was not leaving till the end of the year, and I was at present a supernumerary; perhaps I ought to explain to Catholics that the Anglican diaconate usually lasts a whole year, so that I had not as yet the burdens or the privileges of the priesthood. I read the services in chapel in my turn; some eccentricities in the rendering of these disquieted the President at first, but they involved no matter of principle, and I yielded, I hope not too ungraciously. The only matter of contention that remained was the rapidity with which I did my part; this habit, though I sometimes tried to meet the occasional protests of my colleagues, I cannot say that I ever mastered. I dare say I went too fast; but personally I have a loathing of carefully mouthed enunciation in church. I do not think I am alone in the caprice.

The Anglican deacon, from the first, occupies the pulpit as if he were a priest: my own preaching was not confined to, and indeed did not begin at, Trinity Chapel. My second sermon was in an Oxford parish church, and was supposed to be an appeal for foreign missions; I am afraid it must have sounded more like a condemnation of them. I never shared the view of some ultra-correct clergymen who held that Anglicanism (like anti-clericalism) was "not for export"; that only a geographical and historical accident had separated us from Latin Christendom, and that we should hold ourselves responsible for our own flocks, leaving evangelization to Rome; in the Dominions at least, and among our own flesh and blood, it seemed to be natural that our own variety of religion should extend

its sway. But I was in a fever of revolt against moderation and half-heartedness. Taking my text from the
miracle at Cana, I condemned as " water " the official
doctrines which so many of our missionaries preached,
and I went so far as to contrast these missionaries
unfavourably with St. Francis Xavier, whose day it
was. I suppose it was not a felicitous utterance, nor
were others of the same date : it does not do to be at
once very revolutionary in one's sentiments and col-
loquial in one's style to the verge of frivolity. It was
only by degrees that I gained the *entrée* even to the
more " advanced " Anglican pulpits, though one or
two priests were very kind in welcoming me from
the first, the Rector of St. Anne's, Manchester, in
particular.

In Trinity Chapel, though I was not at any great
pains to curb the exuberances of my natural levity, I
did always try to assume less agreement on the part of
my audience, and restrict my subject-matter to plain
doctrines, Communion and Confession especially.
But even in this my success was limited, and an undergraduate (afterwards not only my friend but my
penitent) declared excitedly after my first sermon,
" Such fun ! The new Fellow's been preaching heresy
—all about Transubstantiation." Everywhere I was
conscious that my views did not quite " go down,"
but fortunately I had too much capacity for laughing at myself to fall into the error of posing as a
martyr.

And indeed I had little reason to complain, for,
views or no views, the world was generous to me per-

sonally, and I had no difficulty in making friends.
Dinners in the Old Bursary, where the staid portraits
of Trinity men long dead seemed to look down scan-
dalized on the frivolity of a later generation—or did
they know the ordeal that lay before that generation,
and rejoice that from us the shadow was still hidden ?
—dining and bathing parties in the Long Bridges backwater, convoyed in a flotilla of punts, long Wednesday
evenings when the interval ailments of motor-bicycles
were discussed exhaustively among heaps of banana-
skins—all these were, I am afraid, a very indirect form
of paving the way for evangelical effort, but they certainly awarded the labourer his hire. *Fulsere vere
candidi tibi soles.*

I was now in full work, lecturing and taking pupils.
My earliest subjects for lecturing were Homer and
Virgil, though I did not actually begin my course on the
latter till autumn, 1912. Of the effects of Homeric
study I shall have more to say in the next chapter ;
Virgil—or at any rate the Aeneid—I had never learned
to value before : it was only when I was forced to
look below the surface that I lost my heart to him.
Of the sixth book I managed to make a lecture almost
completely devoted to Purgatory ; otherwise it was
a merely literary delight that I took in the poem ; I
did not hunt for omens.

I was not at leisure to read so elaborately for the
priesthood as for the diaconate, and my only study
outside the prescribed course was the greater part of
Volume I of Tanquerey's *Theologia Moralis.* The
book which interested me above all others in the pre-

scribed course itself was Gairdner on the history of the English Church in the sixteenth century. The author, though he afterwards came to "hold views" about the Reformation, had approached the subject in an entirely impartial spirit, and in this book he had described the steps which preceded the Reformation and accompanied its establishment in a light which, despite my own sympathies, I had never seen them before. I do not know why this should have been so, for I cannot think the book introduced new points of view to my notice, but it took hold of my imagination, and, more than ever, I saw the Reformation as a disaster.

But there was something else to learn besides bookwork; I must know how to "say Mass." My principle was simply to learn to say Mass as a Catholic priest does, with O'Callaghan's translation of Zualdi; when I had once got my model, I could modify it, on the lines of the Prayer Book modifications of it, so as to minister in English to Anglican congregations. I will not weary my readers by entering into vexed questions about the manner (or rather manners) of celebrating the Communion Service customary among Anglicans of my school; my own principle was, whenever I spoke aloud, to use the language of the Prayer Book, when I spoke *secreto*, to use the words ordered by the Latin missal. Of any serious "disloyalty to the Prayer Book" I do not accuse myself, unless that is involved in the shortening of the service by omissions which have become, or are on the way to become, a matter of custom : for such omissions I felt that the circum-

stance of frequent and daily celebrations gave sufficient
warrant.

My summer vacation was spent largely at Caldey,
this time in the guest house, on a reading party with
the Rev. N. P. Williams and one or two others. For
a fortnight or so before my ordination I went, for
quiet though not actually for retreat, to stay with the
Rev. A. H. Baverstock at Hinton Martell in Dorset.
The Ordination retreat was held at Cuddesdon, where
the new Bishop, Dr. Gore, was now installed. The
Bishop went through our examination papers with us,
so far as they concerned doctrine, and questioned me
on one or two points to his own satisfaction, though
I knew that he already regretted the " mediæval "
tendencies of my theology. The Ordination itself took
place at St. Giles's Church, Reading. The Bishop celebrated in a chasuble, the preacher was the Rev. V. S. S.
Coles, whom I had known so well at Pusey House;
the church itself was one where the Divine mysteries
held their proper place in worship, and ceremonial was
used of a kind that in a northern diocese would have
been considered very advanced. It seemed impossible
to believe that less than half a century before all the
accessories of the ceremony would have been condemned as disloyal by almost every bishop on the
bench.

Two days later, on Tuesday, September 24th, the
Feast of our Lady of Ransom, I celebrated for the first
time at St. Mary's Church, Graham Street. I was, of
course, quite unconnected with it, but the vicar, the
Rev. J. C. Howell, then and afterwards a true friend

to me and a model for my priestly ambitions, gladly let me hold the service there : there were cards, and bouquets, and all the accessories of a first Mass ; many of my friends were there, including my brother, who was at that time wholly unacquainted either with the church or with the kind of ceremonies practised there. The rest of the time before the beginning of term I spent at the Trinity Mission in West Ham. From the first, I regarded it as a natural part of my devotions as a priest to say Mass daily, or as nearly that as possible ; from the Trinity Mission I had to travel for three-quarters of an hour to find a church where my manner of celebrating, then perhaps more reminiscent of the missal than of the Prayer Book, was tolerated even in a Mass of devotion.[1] I soon learned to trim my sails to some extent, though I confess that, with the variety of usage which distinguished various churches up and down the country, I had a continual feeling of being on tenterhooks whenever I celebrated at a strange altar. At Oxford, where sisterhoods are plentiful, I found it possible, through the kindness of various institutions, to be at the altar every day except on Wednesdays, when a college meeting stood in the way. At Trinity, I naturally had to arrive at a sort of *concordat* with the President ; I only celebrated there on the " Red-letter " Saints' days.

I only mention these apparently pettifogging troubles

---

[1] About this time I celebrated at a community chapel. One of the brethren was heard to declare afterwards that if he had known what I was going to do he would have got up and stopped me.

because I suppose they contributed to making me feel
rather a pariah in the Church of England. Indeed, I
once told a friend that Anglican churches were divided into those where I wasn't asked to preach and
those where I wasn't allowed to say Mass. A college
don is naturally a nomadic creature ; so far as mere
residence goes, he is on his holiday during a rather
larger part of the year than not : consequently he is
continually visiting new places and strange churches,
and is easily secured as a festival preacher. Reckoning
them up, I find that I have preached in something
between fifty and sixty Anglican pulpits—roughly
speaking, a fresh pulpit for every month of my active
ministry. But at this first stage, when I had not yet
that eminent title to respect, the authorship of a book,
I was not infrequently conscious that my doctrines
and my behaviour were regarded as eccentric. Yet
I do not think I ever doubted that I was "right
where I was." The only thing I can recall which
points in another direction is that from time to time,
when I was making acts of resignation after the models
laid down by the Venerable Father Baker, I used
always to resign myself to the possibility of having to
make my submission to Rome, if that should be God's
will for me. But I thought of this only as a remote
possibility, mentioning it in the same breath with the
possibility that God might wish me to be a religious,
or a foreign missionary—Father Baker encourages
the practice of reconciling oneself to remote contin-
gencies. I was "right where I was," even when not
"happy where I was " ; indeed, Mr. Raper, when

asked by a Catholic friend why I did not " come over " to the Church, was kind enough to suggest that " I was afraid of being too comfortable if I did so." Certainly to be in a small minority does make some demands on the ascetic faculty, but to be permanently amused at yourself lightens the strain considerably.

It was, however, almost immediately after my ordination to the priesthood that a stray literary venture not only marked me out in Oxford itself, but even gave me a certain public outside. At the Friday luncheon parties I have described above much of the conversation used to turn upon the question of a forthcoming book, which was to give a fresh " restatement " of theology according to the opinions then fashionable in Oxford, just as *Lux Mundi* had done in an earlier generation. Mr. Neville Talbot, Mr. Parsons, Mr. Brook, Mr. Rawlinson, and Mr. Moberly were all my boon companions of Friday, and were among the authors ; Mr. Streeter had only just vacated his place by matrimony, and Mr. William Temple, then headmaster of Repton, was a friend of the symposium and of my own. Thus, by personal association, I was in the very centre and stronghold of the movement which produced *Foundations* (as the book was called) ; meanwhile, I gathered in conversation that the theological colour of the book, so far as doctrinal orthodoxy was concerned, would not be my own. Mr. Thompson of Magdalen had recently published a work on the Gospel miracles which had made some stir by its departure from traditional ideas ; the new book was to reprove such excesses, but at the same time was to present to the public a moderately " liberal " statement. Further, it was not difficult from that inside point of view to realize that the *Foundations* camp was not wholly at one ; it had its Right, its Left, and its Centre, like other movements, and compromises very necessary to include Mr. Talbot and Mr. Streeter between the same covers.

Ever since I can remember, or at least since the age of seven, I have been possessed with the devil of lampooning ; my family, my friends both at my private school and at Eton, my Balliol contemporaries, my fellow-missioners at Blackpool, had all inspired me with subjects for *pasquinade*. It was natural that the present situation should appeal to the same instinct ; to know a public character in private life is to be inflamed with the desire of caricaturing him. I cannot remember at what moment it was that the idea, long unconfessed to anybody, came into my head. The multitudinous activities of Mr. Temple suggested a comparison with Dryden's " Zimri " in *Absalom and Achitophel*, and the first few lines I wrote were a close parody of that original ; it proved impossible, however, to carry the close parody further. But the idea stuck in my head, travelled with me, beguiled my hours when I had to wait at a railway-station or lay sleepless in bed. At Caldey especially, in the summer of 1912, it hammered itself out into solid form, and by the time *Foundations* was published in the autumn I had a whole poem in the manner of Dryden ready before me, a description (by mere guess-work, for I had seen no proofs) of the lines on which the book

itself was written and the parts played by the various
contributors; it proved not inaccurate. I meditated
private circulation, but the perpetual hunger of the
Oxford Magazine for copy, to which I was often sacrificed, induced me to print it before showing it to the
authors themselves. I submitted it for correction to
Mr. N. P. Williams, and one or two passages were
excised or toned down : the original form has since
been printed, but was not made public at the time.
The publication of my poem was actually anterior to
the appearance of the book, and this lent it an added
interest.

The lines of it were simple ; it began with a hasty
sketch of the modernizing tendency in the Church of
England since the Reformation ; it then appealed to
the Muse in the classical manner for the names and
qualifications of the seven heroes, alluded in passing
to two well-known Liberal writers who did *not* contribute, and proceeded to give a brief account of each
author and the tendencies of his contribution. The
names were, of course, hidden under Biblical or quasi-
Biblical aliases, just as in Dryden ; Mr. Temple, for
instance, who had been known at Rugby as "the
Bull," I called "Og" after the King of Bashan,
famous in the Old Testament for its bulls. The whole
was *castigatus ad unguem*, there was not a line that I
had not weighed and turned over scrupulously ; it was
as faithful as I could made it to Dryden both in spirit
and in style. I fancy that long practice in writing
Latin elegiacs is good preparation for the studied
balance and carefully weighted emphasis of the

I

heroic couplet. For epigrammatic expression it is an unrivalled vehicle, and such lines as

> For Daniel's blood the critick Lions roar'd,
> And trembling hands threw Jonah overboard,

or,

> When suave Politeness, temp'ring bigot Zeal,
> Corrected *I believe* to *One does feel*,

were easy to catch up and to requote.

The *Oxford Magazine*, though all dons read it,[1] has not, I suppose, a large circulation as papers go ; still, if you miss the πολλοὶ, you reach the χαρίεντες. I think the first inkling I had that I had done anything unusual was being congratulated, *sans phrase*, by the President when I came to High Table that night ; as an expert in examinations, he was not lavish with his Alpha's. The *Magazine* sold out, and the poem was reprinted in a fresh issue ; this also soon became impossible to obtain. The poem was reprinted afterwards in a collection of recent Oxford verse, and, considerably later, I allowed it to be published separately as a sort of tract by the Society of SS. Peter and Paul. The most gratifying circumstance was that the *Magazine*, which ordinarily has no money to waste on light verse, departed so far from its principles as to pay me for it. Somehow, in spite of its restricted circulation, its influence travelled far ; the *Times* newspaper puts it down to my credit, and allows it to hide a multitude of sins, and a whole year later a contributor to the *Church Times* complained that if he ever asked a

---

[1] "What is that paper? You know, the dons' '*Varsity*." So a Trinity man described it in my hearing. (The '*Varsity* is very much the organ of the undergraduates.)

clerical colleague whether he had read *Foundations*, the answer was " No, but I've read a poem about it by a man called Knox."

It was not, I hope, in a personally unkindly spirit that the satire was meant ; certainly it was not so taken by the objects of it. Two days after its appearance I had a post card from Repton inscribed with the words " Ta for puff. Og " ; Dr. Rashdall was reported to me as hugely delighted ; Mr. Thompson, to whom I had been less kind, sent mé a note of personal explanation, and the contributors generally were too well satisfied with the treatment of one another to resent the treatment of themselves. But inevitably the whole thing was treated in orthodox circles as a pamphlet, and I as a champion ; the Old Guard of Tractarianism began to look more kindly on me. My lot was cast, as if in spite of myself, with the obscurantists, long before I had read *Foundations* or been able to get a clear idea of what it was aiming at.

In the Lent of this year an incident happened which might have been expected (which ought, for all I know) to have had a profound effect on me. The Community at Caldey, after trying to induce the Bishop of Oxford to act as their visitor, and meeting with demands from him which they felt they could not conscientiously accept, determined (with some exceptions) to make their submissions to the Church. The news was communicated to me one morning over the telephone by Mr. Carey, of Pusey House ; and from his alarmed tone I guessed that he thought (others certainly thought) that it would be a severe blow to

my Anglicanism. At the moment, the sudden illness
of a great friend at Trinity (he had fallen ill that
morning) left me quite numb to all other sensations.
Later the Abbot sent me a printed document containing the whole correspondence ; and, looking into
it at leisure, though I understood Caldey's attitude
and did not particularly blame them, I saw no reason
for following their example. More than a year before,
the Abbot had assured me that, if he ever felt bound
to leave the Church of England, it would be in circumstances which (in his view) made it impossible for any
conscientious man of our school to remain in it ; should
such an emergency arise, he would not scruple to " go
up on to the housetops and say, Come out of her,
my people." Now, this was not a crisis of the kind ;
the most that had been proved (even if that had been
proved) was that it was impossible to be a Benedictine
in the Church of England, not that it was impossible
to be a conscientious " Catholic " in the Church of
England. The Abbot had not gone up on to the housetops, or appealed for companions in his change of
allegiance. I do not blame him ; for I myself used
to suppose that only a general landslip could dislodge
me, and I myself found, when the call came, that it
came to me singly. But it is not to be wondered at if
after reading the correspondence I decided, with whatever regret, that it was no business of mine.

I spent Holy Week at the Trinity Mission ; an attack
of influenza following on the sudden necessity of
celebrating four times on Easter Day (apart from
other services) prevented my seeing what would, to

me, have been one of the most impressive sights of my
life—the funeral of Father Stanton, for so many years
curate of St. Alban's, Holborn. It is hard to estimate
that strength has been lent to the extreme position in
the Church of England by those years of devoted
service and almost uninterrupted persecution. "Look
at a man like Father Stanton " is the regular answer
to an attack on Anglican Sacramentalism, whether
from the Protestant side or from the Catholic. To me
especially he was an inspiration, since he was a Trinity
man and in Trinity I had met him when I was an
undergraduate. I devoted my sermon to him on the
next occasion when I was put down to preach in
Trinity Chapel.

By the end of that year I was moving among a fresh
circle of undergraduates, in addition to the banana-
eaters of Wednesday evening. Some were Trinity men,
some from other colleges, especially Balliol and Magdalen : it is hard to give a definition or even a description of them, except perhaps to say that in a rather
varied experience I have never met conversation so
brilliant—with the brilliance of humour, not of wit.
The circle is broken now by distance and by death : I
only mention it here because it was among these that
I first began to make proselytes. At the time of which
I am speaking, two of them already had adopted what
I heard (and shuddered to hear) described as " Ronnie
Knox's religion." Their names are no business of
anybody's, and they will reappear in this book under
the initials B and C. Both were scholars, both had a
certain prominence, the one at the O.U.D.S., and the

other at the Union. The intimacy I formed with them, combined with their adhesion to my religious views, did much at the time to make me feel comfortable in my then position ; and was to do much later, in God's Providence, to make me feel uncomfortable and to quit it.

VIII

IN SEARCH OF DEFINITIONS

Italiam, quam tu jam rere propinquam,
Vicinosque ignare paras invadere portus,
Longa procul longis via dividit invia terris.

I HAVE tried to carry on the chronological sequence
of this book as far as the end of the summer term
of 1913 ; in order to explain the development of the
ideas which I then both formulated to myself and
promulgated in public, I must retrace my steps considerably. From the summer of 1910 onwards my
mind was occupied almost continuously with the place
of authority in religion ; but it must be said at once
that I approached this subject from two quite different
points of view, and the conclusions I formed on
these two lines, though not (I think) inconsistent
with each other, were not consciously brought into
relation.

In the first place, I had to decide for myself, as every
Anglican has to decide for himself when he aspires to
the ministry, how far the traditions of the Church about
the Incarnation, the Resurrection, etc., formally stated
by my own Church with all the clearness, if not with
all the elaborateness, of Catholic definitions, were
binding upon my acceptance ; and to what extent I
was at liberty—and, because at liberty, to some extent

under obligation—to speculate for myself and form my own conclusions. The question, in fact, was one of orthodoxy—how far, as a clergyman, could I be a " Liberal " ? In the second place, holding the views I held about doctrines such as the Sacrifice of the Mass, the sinlessness of our Lady, etc., and knowing such doctrines to be out of harmony with the tendencies of official religion ; mentally committed, moreover, to acquiescence in devotional practices which the officials of my own church tolerated with difficulty or in some cases were endeavouring to exterminate—I had to decide for myself whether I could conscientiously hold office under such superiors without scruples and mental reservations. The question was one of loyalty ;—how far, as a clergyman, could I be a " Romanizer " ? Both questions ultimately bore on the same point, but I hope I have made it clear that the pressure under which I asked them was different in the two cases.

In regard to orthodoxy, my views when I left Eton were orthodox above the average ; my oracle was Mr. G. K. Chesterton—to a large extent he is so still. (I did not acquit him of paradox ; but, after all, what was a paradox but a statement of the obvious so as to make it sound untrue ?) I accepted the paradoxes of my religion as, if anything, a test of its genuineness ; not on any barren principle of *credo quia impossibile*, but on the ground that the kind of doctrine which shows less signs of having been tampered with by rationalism is likely to represent the least contaminated tradition about the deposit of faith. At Balliol, under the influence of other people's difficulties, I tended to lower my standards and be content with minimizing interpretations of the doctrines I stoutly championed. This process was arrested by Greats, which demanded the employment of my thoughts on philosophy rather than theology, and, when I returned to Oxford, there was no exterior reason (as far as I can see) why my views should not have developed in one direction as much as in another.

The occasion of my discovering which way my mind was pointing may be thought a frivolous one. It is part of the functions of a don to read papers to undergraduate societies; it is part of the wisdom of a don to realize that, in a society where *homines homines velut unda supervenit unam*, the same paper may be read any number of times without being hailed as an old friend. I thought I would write two; one for theological societies on St. Paul, one for secular societies on Sherlock Holmes. The latter was written first, and the former then proved unnecessary. I had no sooner read my Sherlock Holmes paper (about the end of 1910) than I realized that it would do for theological societies as well—it was interpreted as a tract.

There was no particular reason why it should have been—I had no clear idea what sort of criticism I was setting out to satirize. A colleague suggested to me afterwards that I must have had in mind A. C. Bradley's interpretations of Shakespeare. Thus, I divided up the Holmes story as a form of literary art into eleven characteristic divisions, each with its Greek name, and showed how more were present in some stories,

fewer in others. I gave an elaborate study of Holmes'
view of life, and a still more elaborate study of Dr.
Watson's. I declared Watson's bowler hat to be a
symbol of almost religious significance. But I did
also invent a whole controversy, diversified with the
names of various imaginary German scholars, on the
question of the authenticity of several stories, showing
the reasons for pronouncing some of them, on internal
evidence, to be the work of a different hand. The
paper was read to at least three societies in Oxford,
and one in London. It was published in a magazine
(*The Blue Book*), edited chiefly by undergraduates,
and won me the privilege of a letter from Sir Arthur
Conan Doyle himself, who did not quite seem to have
realized that the criticism was not meant to be serious.
But in theological Oxford it was taken as an attack
on the methods of the Higher Criticism, and I found
myself already stamped as an opponent of that tendency.

I was aroused against it in earnest as the result of
preparation for delivering lectures on the Iliad. I read
Prof. Murray's *Rise of the Greek Epic*, and Andrew
Lang's reply to it, Professor Geddes, Miss Stawell, Dr.
Leaf's notes and introductions, the text itself, and
finally one or two handbooks. I looked up all the
references, balanced all the arguments, checked all the
contradictions. I must not weary my readers with
technical stuff ; but this is what I principally noticed.
Prof. Murray, Prof. Geddes, and Dr. Leaf all agreed
that the Iliad was composite, but they did not in the
least agree as to which were the early parts and which

the late ; moreover, Miss Stawell came in and further
troubled their reckonings.   Now, if one critic says A
is late and B is early, while another says A is early and
B is late, and so on throughout, you may believe
either, but not both, and you begin to have suspicions
that it is safer to believe neither.   And then you read
the handbooks, and find that the gentlemen who wrote
these assume Prof. Geddes' division in one place and
Dr. Leaf's in another, without the smallest consciousness of inconsistency.   Sir Richard Jebb did not seem
to me guiltless of this last charge, but the handbook
with which, above all, I broke spears was, I regret to
say, the work of a member of the Society of Jesus,
Fr. Browne, of Dublin.

Now, when I had reached the conviction that the
internal evidence for splitting up the Iliad was not
strong enough to hang a dog on, except in these cases
where (it so happened) there was external evidence in
antiquity for suspecting a difference of authorship,
I began to be a little distrustful of critics and of handbooks altogether.   And when I came to read the books
on the Old Testament I have already mentioned as
part of my preparation for my deacons' papers, a
curious analogy caused me misgivings.   I was only
reading the handbooks, and even if I could have read
the original critics themselves (by learning German) I
could not have got at my original documents without
learning Hebrew.   All the *petitiones principii*, the
splitting up of books into various strata of authorship
on the ground of criteria arbitrarily assumed, and then
suspecting interpolations everywhere merely in order

to make the facts square with the theories, were in evidence here as in my Homeric authors—only I could not check the process. And I began to be less afraid when my handbooks talked to me about "the consensus of expert opinion," and "the assured results of modern criticism."

With the New Testament I was on my own ground once more. Scott on the Fourth Gospel never seemed to me to state a general rule about his subjects to which I could not at once adduce a stultifying quantity of exceptions ; I plastered the book with corrections. Schweitzer was even more provocative ; moreover, he was a pet of the Oxford theologians, who saw in his theory that Jesus of Nazareth was a fanatic (and not far from a lunatic) a dexterous counter to the old German argument that he was merely a sublime moral teacher. I wrote an examination of Schweitzer's assumptions in the form of a pamphlet which I had been asked to write for a series ; it was not accepted, being probably badly written as well as over-orthodox. But my doubts about the Higher Criticism were redoubled, I fell into a horrible scepticism, in which at times I lost all lively faith in the existence of Q. I could not accept the disbeliefs which the theologians propounded for my acceptance. If I was to go to heaven with the Higher Critics, it must be on the plea that invincible ignorance blinded me to the light of doubt.

And then, to complete my pitiable case, the college wanted me to lecture on Logic. It is quite true that lecturing on elementary Logic for Pass Moderations—

it is very elementary—did not introduce me to any profound laws of reasoning of which I had hitherto been unaware. But to invent, for the instruction of youth, instances which show the use and abuse of various reasoning processes, does make you alive to the manifold possibilities of error, does put you on your guard in your ordinary reading, so that you check every argument you meet and test its validity. In a word, I began to despair of my intellect, not because it was so fallible, not because it sinned against faith, not because it tempted me to pride, but because it was so irrepressibly orthodox. The world around me seemed full of people cleverer than myself who lapped up all this liberal theology like well-drilled seminarists, and my mind, with the same data in front of it, was for ever questioning and picking holes. It was all very well to disagree with Prof. Murray about Homer, in spite of my respect for him ; for no eternal issues hung on the criticism of the Iliad. But when I found that I could not accept the German doctrines which claimed the homage of an expert theologian like Mr. Streeter, what was I to do ? Was I to say, I am a heretic because Mr. Streeter believes this ? Or was I to say, Mr. Streeter is a heretic because I, merely because I, think that ?

In this predicament I fell back upon the doctrine that *faith is a gift.* It was a phrase chiefly made familiar to me through its constant repetition by the Rev. V. S. S. Coles, my old oracle at Pusey House : in other ways, I am afraid, the attitude I was adopting did not meet with this approval, but here I frankly own myself his disciple. (I can still see him shouting about the gift of faith down Baron von Hügel's ear-trumpet, with the air of a man getting a difficult trunk call.) If the right orientation of the mind in theological matters depended upon the existence of certain traditional doctrinal formulæ, in which you believed primarily because you co-operated with the grace given you to believe in them, then there was one law for Mr. Streeter and myself and the charcoal-burner, and I need not mind whom I disagreed with, so long as I did not disagree with the Church. I do not mean that I supposed the faith could not be, or ought not to be, defended by rational argument ; very much the contrary ; but I did find in this way certain doctrines which I could preach authoritatively from the pulpit, without the feeling that I was making them rest upon the security of my unaided intellect—an intellect, it seemed, so wholly out of touch with those around it.

" Certain doctrines," for, looking back upon it, I find that although I myself regarded the doctrines of the Church (so far as I apprehended them) as an organic whole, in the pulpit I usually preached as authoritative only the doctrines traditional in the Church of England —the Atonement, the Resurrection, and so on—and argued deductively in favour of doctrines such as Transub tantiation and the Immaculate Conception (the latter, in St. James's, Plymouth, I even deduced logically from the Thirty-nine Articles). My theology was really in two departments, determined by the nature of the opposition against which I was fighting :

against Modernism I argued fundamental doctrines, taking my stand upon tradition, Anglican no less than Catholic: against Protestantism I argued the pious corollaries of the Faith, taking my stand (at least primarily) on deductive reasoning.

In this second department, as I said at the beginning of this chapter, my difficulty was not one of orthodoxy, but one of loyalty to the principles of a not very sympathetic Church. Now, if you are by temperament cautious, and indisposed to make much of supernatural religion, it is easy enough to be a "loyal Anglican," for you have Anglicanism in the soul. But if by temperament you are the opposite of all this, your loyalty, such as it is, becomes a matter of constraint : you have to pull yourself up and ask, " Let me see : am I being loyal ? " And out of that question arises imperiously the more ultimate question " Am I being loyal—*what to ?*"

I knew, of course, that a Catholic does not stop twice to ask whether he is being loyal to the Pope, or the Church, or the traditions of the Church, or to his Bishop, or to the decrees of the Councils—it is all the same to him. But, owing to the paucity and the ambiguity of its title-deeds, and the widely different points of view adopted by its dignitaries, the Church of England allows of no such comfortable confusions— unless, as I say, you are temperamentally Anglican. The commonest way out of the difficulty is to take credit to yourself for " loyalty to the Prayer Book." That I never did claim, for it seemed to me as monstrous as talking about loyalty to the Breviary or the Missal :

it was making man the slave of the instruments ; moreover, it always seemed to me that the ideal opened the door for a quite disastrous (though no doubt honest) elasticity of conscience. On many questions, too, the Prayer Book was either silent, or obstinately oracular, and those who sought its guidance must be prepared for disappointment :

Inconsulti abeunt, sedemque odere Sibyllae.

I hope I shall not be accused here of playing with my subject. Let me put, to admirers of the Prayer Book, a simple question : If a doctor asked you whether it was or was not right to perform a certain obstetric operation, would you dare to say, " Be loyal to the Prayer Book"? And yet two lives are involved.

The other and more obvious solution to the problem is to say, " I will be loyal to my Bishop." Now (I am speaking here entirely for myself, but I suspect that a good many other priests thought with me) in practice this gives rise to an intolerable series of difficulties. Am I to obey my Bishop if he forbids me to wear vestments ? No, not then, says the loyal school, for he is acting *ultra vires*. Judged by what standard ? Your own conscience ? Why, then, invoke authority at all ? Or the Prayer Book ? Then we are a dead Church once more. Or the Bench of Bishops ? But they have not spoken. Or the Bishop in Synod ? But his Synod does not meet. Am I to obey my Bishop if he forbids me to use the Litany of Loretto ? Yes, says the loyal school—but on what theory ?

But I have no need to dilate on these practical difficulties, which are fully recognized by Anglican Bishops themselves : the ordinary way in which Anglican priests avoid them is to appeal from the Bishop, when they disagree with him, to their own idea of what took place in the primitive Church or takes place in the Universal Church. To me, these difficulties never presented themselves, because from the moment I considered the question at all I had a doubt far more ultimate and wholly theoretical.

I was writing a paper to be read to a Church society in Corpus ; it was, if I remember right, in 1911. And if some of my friends have been surprised to hear that in another matter I sat at the feet of the Rev. V. S. S. Coles, they will be still more surprised to learn that in this matter my master was the Dean of Durham.[1] Seldom did a Bishop allow any extreme practice, or forbid any " Evangelical " practice, or attempt to suppress any " Liberal " doctrine, without the brilliant Canon of Westminster (as he was formerly) writing to the papers to ask what right the Bishop had to take such action. The Bishop was a functionary responsible to a legal body, the Church of England, which had fixed laws and could have more to-morrow if Parliament saw fit to pass them ; like a magistrate or a local authority of any kind, he was there to administer the law, not to make it ; he was, in a particular and even a unique department, a servant of the Crown.

Now, in adopting the Dean's view of the episcopate,

[1] Now Bishop of Hereford.

K

I did not follow his conclusions ; he is a law-abiding person, and I am not. I argued that certain laws were laid down, not with any categorical force, but for the protection of society, e.g. the law that you must not ride a bicycle without a lamp after a given time at night. Now, if and in so far as you know that in these particular circumstances (an uphill road over a moor) you will not endanger anybody's safety, you can break the law without any moral delinquency : I am delighted to find that this principle is recognized in one of the most recent Cases of Conscience (ad S. Apollinarem, 4th May, 1914). The same held good, I maintained, of law in the Church of England ; it was not absolute, but represented a sort of contract between you and your parish. If a majority of the active members of your parish agreed with you in wanting (let us say) the ceremonial use of incense, then it did not matter whether it was legal or illegal ; you would take the risks. And whether it was or was not illegal, the Bishop, though he had a right as a legal functionary to set the law in motion, had no right whatever to come and say, "I command you, as your Bishop, to stop doing this." Nor (I would admit) if an Evangelical clergyman had Evening Communion with the consent of his parish, had the Bishop a right, quâ Bishop, to interfere.

Whence, then, did I get any authority at all ? And how could I linger for a day in a State Church of this aggravated description ? My answer was, that for me there was, and for everyone I hoped some day there would be, an authority not enforced by law, but binding absolutely on the conscience—the authority, namely, of all the decrees and traditions which were operative in the English Church in (say) 1500, before the breach with Rome. Some departures from these traditions— especially the marriage of the clergy, the giving of the Chalice to the laity, the use of the vernacular in public worship—one was bound to recognize, but one recognized them, as it were, under protest, as part of the slavery to which the English Church was submitted at the Reformation. To get back to the 1500 stage, with the consent of the laity but undeterred by the fulminations of Bishops, was the great object. And after that ? Well, I was not quite sure.

This was the system of ideas I had in my mind, though I cannot be sure how much of it I put on paper, when I talked to the Corpus Church Society. I am afraid that my ideas of loyalty will remind some of my readers of Hongree, sub-lieutenant of Chassoores, in the *Bab Ballads* :

> Obedience was young Hongree's strongest point ;
> But he imagined that he only owed
> Obedience to his Mahree and his king. . . .
> " But Mahree is asleep in bed, I hope,
> And Charles, my King, a hundred leagues from this,"

and so on. I will only urge that I was attempting to find a *rationale* for a state of affairs which existed all around me. Bishops had been disobeyed, and were disobeyed still ; Faithorn Green had gone to prison, and I was prepared to go to prison myself : priests were trying to reintroduce practices because they were pre-Reformation practices, and their Bishops first hesi-

tated, then were silent, then gave way. The Church
of England was not a static body with fixed ideals,
but a microcosm of conflicting movements, of which
my own was one. I tried to find a logical shape for
principles not peculiar to myself, and at least I did it
openly. Church circles in Corpus sat rather aghast ;
even my friend Mr. Hicks (who afterwards preceded
me into the Church) seemed uncertain how to take it ;
and Mr. Plummer (the Chaplain), commenting on a
quotation I had made from Acts xxxvii. 27, suggested
that I might have gone on to the fourteenth verse
of the next chapter—" And so we went towards
Rome."

This was while I was still a layman ; naturally I
was anxious not to leave any misapprehension about
my ideas when I aspired to the diaconate. I therefore
asked for an interview with Dr. Paget : he invited me
to stay at Cuddesdon, and there I told him that I had
this difficulty about episcopal authority—namely, that
I felt any obedience I showed to him would be dictated
either by personal respect or by acquiescence in his
decision as in that of a purely legal official ; I could
not give him obedience in the sense in which a Roman
Catholic priest gave it to a Roman Catholic Bishop.
These were not mere words : for my dream of the
Church of England was a dream for the future, which
I did not hope to see in my lifetime : I was not medi-
tating any particular act of insubordination, and could
indeed conceive of many circumstances in which a
personal respect for a bishop or a threat of law would
circumscribe my actions (the Bishop himself had

recently set the law in motion against Mr. Henly, of
Wolverton, now a Catholic priest at Littlehampton).
It was on the point of theory, not of practice, that I
wished to make myself clear. Rather to my surprise,
Dr. Paget found no difficulty in accepting my delibera-
tion, which he did with the utmost kindness. Yet in
point of fact it is hard to see how an Anglican bishop,
however little he loved Erastianism, could take exception to the theory.

All this, except my lecturing on logic, belongs to the
period immediately before my diaconate, before the
summer of 1911. It must have been, I think, during
my diaconate that it seemed probable I should have to
tackle the question of authority, no longer from
isolated points of view but with a single clear grasp,
in order to contribute an article on it to a book. It was
at the time when *Foundations* was in preparation ;
and it was with no sense of direct rivalry, but with the
idea that there was room for a similar book on more
traditional lines, that Father Figgis, of the Community
of the Resurrection, Mirfield, tried to collect a joint
board of authorship from among the rising intellects
of Oxford and Cambridge. Nothing came of the pro-
ject in the end, but I remember Fr. Figgis coming
up to Oxford to talk it over, and I remember discussing
my own subject, that of Authority, with Mr. Spens,
of Corpus, Cambridge. It is characteristic, I am
afraid, of the way my memory works that I can remember the precise place at which the conversation ter-
minated, as I let him out of the dark passage that leads
out of Trinity at the back into the lamp-lit spacious-

ness of St. Giles'—I can remember all that, without remembering precisely our points of difference. I think he was urging the view that the Church was not simply an organization which from time to time turned out a set of infallible decrees, at Jerusalem, at Nicea, and so on, but a body inspired with an infallible instinct or tendency which makes naturally for orthodoxy the whole time. I think now that there is a good deal to be said for that way of looking at it when you know where to find your church: my objection to all such views at the time was that when once you got to the Reformation you had either to capitulate to Rome, as the sole current of the infallible instinct, or else to allow that the instinct diffused itself over a wide morass of reformed and unreformed sects, some of them bearing evident signs of stagnation. I preferred, therefore, a narrowly Conciliar view, such as was that of the Tractarians, and such as I (falsely, I found) imagined to be the view current in Anglican Sacramentalist circles. Now, Conciliar views have an unfortunate tendency to differ according to the number of Councils you recognize as ecumenical, but they have this in common—that you tie down the definitions of the faith to a series of definite points in history; that their sanction consists in a series of majority votes, behind which you recognize the promised guidance of the Holy Spirit; that the body of truth so defined cannot now be added to, until the scattered portions of the Church are reunited in one Society.

This was the doctrine I intended to set forth, but I

must have been conscious that in doing so I should have to cross swords definitely with the Roman theory, and I do not think that at the time I arrived at any conclusion as to the amount of primacy or authority which, in cold print and with a full sense of responsibility, I should accord to the See of Peter. But one evening, coming back from Trinity Common-room, my mind warmed with the excellent conversation and my body with the excellent port of that institution, I sat down and wrote what was to be the concluding paragraph of my essay. When I found that it could not fulfil its original purpose, I turned it into the concluding paragraph of a sermon, preached on Royal Martyr Day at St. Cuthbert's, Philbeach Gardens, and afterwards printed. The sermon was chiefly devoted to repeating the point of view I had taken up in the paper I have mentioned above, read to the Corpus Church Society ; at the end, it fell upon the mention of Rome, and the adjustable conclusion fitted in well enough. I quote it here, partly because it was misunderstood by some people as flat Romanism, partly because if carefully read it shows how far I was from Rome.

" Mother-like she calls us, truant children, and we, conscious of no wayward disobedience, but of an interior guidance that does not readily give up its secret to the hard categories of logical surrender, still cling to our frantic separation, in the hope of a richer and fuller Reunion in the years to come. Looking round us, we dare not claim to be a natural and healthy branch of the heavenly Vine, but we do claim that in

our half-severed branch the sap has not altogether
ceased to flow. To our view, Rome too has pretensions
to abate, and wrongs to confess, before the heart of
England can understand her. Sorrowing she calls us,
like that Mother of old, who sought her son and could
not find him, as he sat refuting the doctors in the
Temple ; but we too must be about our Father's business, though we meet our Mother again only after a
Gethsemane ; it may be, a Calvary. And surely we
dare not doubt that . . . the Church of England
will once again be builded on the Rock she was
hewn from, and find a place, although it be a place of
penitence and of tears, in the eternal purposes of
God."

Now, it seems to me that in this passage I took up
a quite definitely anti-Roman point of view. Rome
had " pretensions to abate "—I do not quite know
what claims I meant ; probably the bull on Anglican
orders was uppermost in my mind, but I do not think
I should have stopped there. Rome had pretensions
to abate, and when we had restored the Church of
England to what it was (apart from the Papacy) before
the Reformation, and Rome had abated (I probably
would have said) the full Infallibility claim, each side
would be in a position to join hands with the other,
and a real, corporate reunion would be the result.
Meanwhile, to me as to the rest of my school, any
individual submission to Rome was a set-back for the
Corporate Reunion movement, and consequently to
be deplored.

It was in the summer of 1913 that I was led to express myself publicly both on the place of authority in religious belief, and on the position of the Church of England as against the rest of Christendom, in the circumstances which I am to describe in the next chapter.

IX

SCIOMACHY

Talia vociferans sequitur, strictumque coruscat
Mucronem, nec ferre videt sua gaudia ventos.

THE present chapter must deal with the publication of two books, or, more correctly speaking, of
a book and a tract. The sermons which went to form the
tract in its original shape were preached while the book
was being written, and the tract itself preceded the
book in the time of its appearance : a strictly chronological treatment would result in a hopeless confusion
of the issues in question. I make no apology, therefore, for separating the two subjects entirely, though
both belong to the summer of 1913, and explaining,
first, the circumstances surrounding the production of
the tract.

It all arose from a remark of Mr. Mackay's (Vicar
of All Saints', Margaret Street). In an unguarded
moment he had said to me, " It is quite time that somebody like you or Williams wrote a book explaining
exactly what you stand for." It must be plain to my
readers that his " or " was in this case an *aut* rather
than a *vel*. But it was to me the remark was made, and
it stuck in my head when the Rev. R. H. Miers, of
St. James's, Plymouth, asked me to preach a course of
sermons in what may be called the height of the Ply-

mouth season, the first half of August. Two of my
friends, Mr. Child and Mr. Baker, were then Mr. Miers'
curates, with a mission chapel more specially in their
charge, and it seemed I might combine business with
pleasure by spending part of my holiday under their
roof and preaching at St. James's on the Sundays. The
fixture was arranged, and the subject I ultimately
chose for my sermons was " The Church of England,
Past, Present, and Future."

Earlier in the summer I paid another visit to Belgium, this time with my brother, who now shared my
religious views, with Mr. Wickham, of St. John's,
Bovey Tracey, and Mr. Lyon, of Middlecot—a house
overlooking Bovey from the edge of the moor. If I
have not already mentioned my friendship with Mr.
Lyon and my visits to Middlecot, it is because I made
them so often that they had become almost a part of
my everyday experience : I cannot remember any
topic in religion, politics, society, literature, or (Heaven
help me) art which I have not discussed with Mr. Lyon
or his guests, sprawling before a wood fire in that ample
chimney corner. Once again, my fellow-travellers were
as ready as myself to appreciate not only the religion
of Belgium but the forms in which it expressed itself.
We made the same round—Bruges, Ypres, Brussels,
Antwerp, Namur, Dinant, Bruges again and always
Bruges ; if I had lost any of my fervid belief in the
religion of Belgium as a working religion which must
be transplanted to English soil, this visit revived it.
It was Benediction at St. John the Baptist's, Namur,
that I described to my Plymouth congregation when

I tried to paint them the picture of what the Church of England was to be.

My visit to Plymouth was more in the nature of a house-party than of a missionary journey. Mr. Gurney was there, accompanied by the huge Talbot car which was familiarly referred to as " the Light Ford " ; two of my Trinity friends were there ; B, whom I have already mentioned, was one of them. Our days were spent largely in bathing and motoring ; at night cool airs and the reflection of lights on the bay encouraged, it must be confessed, conversation rather than work. In these circumstances I prepared my sermons with difficulty and at haphazard. Doubtless I ought to have written them on my knees at a prie-dieu : actually, my memories are of typewriting furiously in a strong through draught, with Mr. Child shouting to me to get ready and come out. Perhaps my preaching gained in spontaneity, and if it lost in polish, I do not think it was guilty of irresponsible thought. The sermons were reported (in abstract) by the local press, and arrangements had also been made for the printing of them by the Society of SS. Peter and Paul.

This Society had come into existence not very long before, and I am responsible for it to the extent that it was I who in the first place introduced the capital to the enterprise. Its activities had hitherto been confined to the production of liturgical works, designed to standardize the ritual and ceremonial of the extreme party (a felt want) by an adaptation of the principles laid down by the Congregation of Rites. A Missal had already been issued ; a Breviary was in preparation. But this was to be the Society's first departure in the way of polemical literature. Its exterior was, not wholly by accident, white and yellow in colour. The text it bore on the outside, which afterwards became the hallmark of a series, was *Loquere filiis Israel ut proficiscantur;* the last word (which ribaldry translated " go over ") is " go forward " in the Authorised Version—a reference to an E.C.U. speech of Mr. Underhill's (Vicar of St. Alban's, Birmingham) in which he demanded a forward movement and, what was then an innocuous phrase, " a place in the sun." The three sermons were first to appear as a separate brochure, and then in a distended form, accompanied by other inflammatory utterances of mine in the last two years.

Meanwhile, the sermons had to be preached. I suppose I must have had congregations of about eight hundred, and it was not a " picked " congregation such as one associates with churches of the kind : it had a considerable outside element, for Plymouth was full of visitors and the church is close to the station. I have no idea what they thought of me ; certainly they listened, and I think only one person " went out." I was preaching at Evensong, and took my three texts from the first lesson of the service in each case— Naboth's vineyard was the story of the Reformation ; the mantle of Elias with which Eliseus divided the River Jordan was the Catholicism which still worked in the days of Pusey as in the days of Wolsey ; the noble who doubted the power of God to raise the siege of Samaria was the pessimist who doubted the possibility of corporate reunion with Rome. I must, I am afraid, give a fairly detailed account of the views I worked out. I argued as follows:

The Reformation was the usurping by the Crown of the administrative rights previously enjoyed by the Papacy. The circumstances of the change were atrocious on both sides; the effect was that a large spiritual " connection " (as we talk of " a business connection ") changed hands. More and Cranmer did not die for the sake of two separate churches respectively, but for the sake of this single spiritual connection—each of them for his idea of what it ought to be. The Reformation did not unchurch the Church; it merely put the Church into a state of Babylonish captivity under the Crown. In order to keep the peace, Queen Elizabeth and her advisers botched together a series of provisional formulas—doctrinal and liturgical—midway between the two parties in tendency. These formulas, which we call the " Reformation settlement," were a *pis aller*, a *faute de mieux ;* nobody wanted them, everybody hoped they would change when a monarch of more decided views came in. It was the seventeenth century, with its Puritan persecution, which made Englishmen think of the Reformation settlement as an end in itself. It was the eighteenth century, with its combination of Latitudinarianism and Erastianism, that made the Church of England " inclusive " of divergent doctrines. It was the nineteenth century, with the gradual abandonment by Parliament of its legal claim to tyrannize over the Church, which unconsciously and as it were by accident

put administrative power into hands it was never
meant for—the hands of the Bishops. (Here I developed the point made in my paper at Oxford, that
the jurisdiction of Anglican Bishops was a usurped
prerogative.) And my conclusion was, that if the
Church of England had already changed so many times
over, it was not the part of "loyalty" to preserve it
in situ; an Anglican must have his vision of what his
church ought to be, and must work to make that vision
come true. So far the first sermon.

The second sermon was, generally speaking, an
attack on those moderating influences in the Church
of England which I had hated so long. The Bishops
were engaged in an effort to make a Procrustean bed
out of the Establishment, levelling up in some places
and levelling down in others so as to reduce us all to a
single standard of mediocrity. The characteristic
marks of this standard I defined as "green stoles and
bad brass and the Church of England Men's Society,
and the Holy Eucharist at eight and Matins at eleven,
and Confession if you happen to feel like it"; and
even if this standard should come to be raised a little,
the official religion would bear the same marks of
pointlessness and restraint. Against this policy of
repression at both ends I raised quite frankly the
standard of revolt; the Bishops had (as I had already
shown) no right to dictate the policy of the Church
according to their own fancy; they must act as legal
officials or not at all. And meanwhile a real enemy
was creeping into the Church, which I described
vaguely as Modernism. Our great danger was the

absence of a living authority to deal with this, and I asserted boldly that if and when the Church of England either gave up the recitation of the Creed *Quicumque vult* (the strongest mark of her orthodoxy), or tampered with the marriage laws so as to countenance divorce, or officially admitted Nonconformists to Communion, it would be a church to which neither I nor my supposedly sympathetic audience could conscientiously continue to belong.

The third sermon began by drawing attention to the desire for reunion which was then making itself felt everywhere; agreeing in this desire, our Church leaders differed as to the direction in which they wanted the process to take place. Rome and Nonconformity were the real alternatives, and we had to decide which company we preferred. Nonconformity was not the "blood-and-thunder" soul-converting religion it used to be; it was tending more and more in practice towards a system which made religion comfortable, whereas the cry of Catholicism was still "Give us our Purgatory now." Rome was hated and persecuted as the Saviour had foretold, and this seemed in itself an indication where our true Orientation lay. But of course there were the people who appealed for reunion with the Orthodox Eastern bodies; these I am afraid I dismissed rather rudely, with some strictures on Tsarism and superstition, but I did also make the clear point that the Greeks themselves regarded us as apostates, cut adrift from their natural patriarch. What, then, of reunion with Rome? Here came in the pessimist, who treated the whole idea as impossible.

To this I replied that nothing was impossible with God ; that Rome might some day (not merely acknowledge our orders, but) retrospectively admit our claim to a continuous existence as a church : as long as we were not compelled to deny that, we could be once more united with her. Till then, individual submissions were a mistake. " It is not for us, the glamour of the seven hills, and the consciousness of membership, living and actual, in the Church of the Ages ; we cannot set our feet upon the rock of Peter, but only watch the shadow of Peter passing by, and hope that it may fall on us and heal us. . . . And yet, even now, we are not left without hope. Our needs have still a place in the compassionate heart of Mary, where she sits by her Father's side ; she has not forgotten her children, just because they have run away from their schoolmaster, and unlearnt their lessons, and are trying to find their way home again, humbled and terrified in the darkness."

I am, naturally, not concerned here to defend either the logical validity or the historical accuracy of the account I thus gave of English Church history. Nor, on the other hand, am I anxious to criticize it here, for that would be to anticipate the movements of my own mind. I only wish to draw attention to a single lacuna in the argument, because it becomes of importance later. In the second of my sermons I quite definitely said that if the Church of England could not get *within the next fifty years* an authority which, speaking with divine assurance, could put an end to the activities of " Modernism," it would become an im-

L

possible place for people of my own school. Now, I
certainly did not mean merely an efficient administra-
tion which *de facto* would be able to combat heresy ; I
meant a centre of authority which could *de jure* pronounce upon errors and condemn them. How on
earth did I expect such a *de jure* authority to be spon-
taneously generated by a Church which had not got
it already ? The only answer on my own principles
would have been that reunion with Rome must come
within fifty years if our Ark was not to be torpedoed
by Modernism, but I am sure I did not mean that.

Whatever I meant, I had certainly given public
expression to the idea that, in certain conceivable
circumstances, secession (in a body) from the Church
of England might become a duty for myself and those
who thought with me. I am not sure why: it might
have been imagined that, on my principles, a "spiritual
connection" which had survived the Reformation
could survive anything ; that no action taken by it,
however public and however official, could compromise
its members. Some of my friends did, later, take a
point of view not far removed from this. Mr. Gurney,
in an inspired moment, when somebody had told him
to pull himself together, replied, " I haven't got any
together " ; we hailed the utterance : perhaps the
Church of England had " not got any together "—
it was not sufficiently an organism to have a vulnerable
centre. I have heard it declared that as long as a
single diocese remained where the Bishop had not
committed himself to, e.g. Arianism, one could continue to work in that diocese as a loyal Anglican and

a loyal Catholic. I could not share this point of view ;
I felt positive that a time might come at which the
Church of England would be unchurched ; yet I never
exactly knew what the symptoms of that time were
to be, on a theory which (as I frankly admitted) only
treated bishops as "confirming and ordaining
machines," not as *de jure* custodians of the deposit of
faith. And I think it would certainly be found that
there are few Anglicans holding strong Sacramental
views who do not admit the concrete possibility that
the Church of England might some day become heretical. " If only," a friend once said to me, " you could
open your *Times* one morning and see a notice to say
that the Church of England has been wound up ! "

In the event of such a crisis (to which I never looked
forward but as to a disaster) I held that it would be
our duty to admit that we had been wrong ; that we
had been misled by appearances into supposing it
God's will that we should labour and suffer for a
desired reunion : and, that admission once made, we
should not feel bound to start a non-juring schism of
our own : we should simply have to look for Catholic
obedience where it obviously could be found—in the
Church of Rome. But so long as God seemed to have
a mission for us in the Church of England, we were
bound to remain where we were.

The house party broke up, and I left Plymouth on
the day after my last sermon to join my family, who
were staying near Tavistock. I think it was the sight
of a newspaper placard at the station, inscribed plainly
with the words " BACK TO ROME," that first made me

realize what an unenviable reputation I might have
been earning myself. I have none of the contramun-
dane in my composition, and I fell easily into a state of
painful depression :

piget incepti, lucisque; suosque
Mutatae agnoscunt, excussaque pectore Juno est.

I had, indeed, already been taken to task by various
friends for publishing, but this was chiefly on the ground
that the ill-considered style of my preaching was not
suited for reproduction in cold print. It was not
literary vanity that now troubled me, it was the
thought of how my friends would take it, of dreary
days of controversy ahead. I saw visions of innumerable breakfast-tables stained, as with a newly spilt
poached egg, by the obtrusive white-and-yellow
manifesto, and I groaned at the idea. At home it did,
in fact, arrive (from a hand more officious than friendly)
one morning of my stay, and the impression it created
was naturally a painful one—all the more so as my
brother, who had now come to share my religious
views, had just declared his intention of being ordained.
As I walked over the moor on Sunday mornings (four
miles each way) to celebrate in the little church at
Mary Tavy, a hideous feeling that none of it was worth
while sometimes oppressed me. Yet I cannot remember a single moment at which individual submission
to Rome occurred to me as a way of escape from my
despondency : I should have regarded it as a cowardly
suggestion if it had.

More than one bishop, I think, was disturbed when
Naboth's Vineyard in Pawn or *The Church in Bondage*

(as the larger publication was called) arrived, forwarded by my unknown benefactors, in his post-box.
The then Bishop of Exeter (Dr. Robertson), an old
Trinity man as well as Bishop of the diocese where my
sermons had been delivered, wrote to me most kindly
about it, but made it a stipulation of my preaching in
his diocese again that I should apply for his special
permission beforehand. Dr. Gore contented himself
with telling me in conversation that he had disliked it.
From several official quarters, as well as from " loyal "
Anglican circles, I heard side-winds of disapproval.
Indeed, a friend who aspired a little later to be bap-
tized as an Anglican, when he pleaded me as an
authority for strong Romanophil tendencies, was
told that my views could be tolerated in one already
ordained, but were not a good recommendation for
admission. I must, however, here as everywhere,
record my gratitude for the extraordinary kindness
and leniency I everywhere experienced. Among those
who shared my views, as well as among a certain irre-
verent undergraduate public, the book had some vogue ;
I heard phrases out of it repeated with relish and even
saw them in print : I think I ought to add that, for
good or ill, the book did " make a difference " to some
people.

I had another brush with authority, less personal
than this. I had, some time before, joined a devotional sodality called the " Catholic League " ; I was
at no time a very active member, for I have a horror
of shilling subscriptions and weekly collects (I never
belonged to any of the ordinary " High Church "

societies). That summer it held a sort of devotiona picnic at Corringham in Essex, with every circumstance of Mariolatry : the vicar, a prudent man, lent his church for the occasion and went away for the day. Consequently, when the Bishop of St. Alban's was informed, he could not get the usual satisfaction out of the local incumbent, who pleaded ignorance of the details ; and he took the unusual step of declaring that he would not ordain or license any member of the Catholic League, or even give him permission to officiate.

It was neither from a scrupulous sense of honesty, nor from any desire to make a fuss, but with genuine curiosity to see whether the Bishop would be as good as his word, that I wrote from Plymouth to explain my position : I was a member of the League, I had not been at the service nor in any way countenanced it ; I was Chaplain of Trinity, and it was customary for the chaplain to give help (as I had done that Holy Week) to the badly understaffed Trinity Mission in West Ham—that is, in the St. Alban's diocese. The reply was perfectly firm ; I must not perform any ministerial function in the diocese unless I would resign from the League. This I refused to do : I was continually being disgusted with the attitude of those priests of my own school who refused to back up a brother-priest when he was attacked—not only refused, but often even joined in the attack by way of advertising their own loyalty :

et, quae sibi quisque timebat,
Unius in miseri exitium conversa tulere.

I would not have this said of me, and I was thus inhibited in the St. Alban's diocese and (when it was divided) in the Chelmsford diocese as well. In the Exeter diocese I could not preach without special permission. And I also refused, from this time onwards, preaching engagements in Manchester, for fear of putting my father into any difficulty thereby. I did not, however, find anything incongruous in my position.

While all this was in progress, I was engaged upon other literary work of a more responsible kind. When I had published my satire in the *Oxford Magazine*, somebody (I think it was Mr. Coles) told me I ought to answer *Foundations* in earnest. About the same time, when I complained to Mr. Howell (of Graham Street) of occasional loneliness and depression, he gave me (as always) excellent advice : " You ought to write a book." It was, quite honestly, in the effort to fill up vacant evenings that I began to write, taking *Foundations* as my subject. In the summer, I showed what I had written to Mr. Howell ; he showed it to Dr. Figgis (of Mirfield), and Dr. Figgis to Messrs. Longmans. I was encouraged to continue, and all through the period I have just been describing I was going at it steadily : it appeared at the autumn publishing season—the anniversary of *Foundations* itself. I had called it *Some Loose Stones*, and the dedication of it was " Sedi Sapientiae," which readers unfamiliar with the Litany of Loretto commonly took to be a reference to the University of Oxford.

It would be difficult to give a proper summary of

the book without being wearisome. It was, in some ways, a statement of the point of view I had arrived at in consequence of my theological reading, as I have described it in the last chapter—namely, that all the speculations of critics are hypotheses, based on *a posteriori* evidence, and, as such, in their very nature uncertain ; for religious purposes certainty is demanded, and if there be any truth in religion, it must depend upon deductions from *a priori* principles, apprehended by the special faculty we call faith. If a conflict arises between these deductions and the inferences we make from *a posteriori* evidence (if, for instance, the Church says that Christ was born of a Virgin and criticism says that He was not) then, unless the issues have been insufficiently cleared up, it must be the deductions from first principles that are right, and the inferences from evidence that are wrong. This was only a single department of my argument, but it was the one generally fastened upon, and let me in for a shower of abuse from my reviewers.

In fact, I dealt with the various parts of *Foundations* separately. I tried to show Mr. Temple that he was in disagreement with the early Fathers, whom he professed to interpret : Mr. Moberly that he was untrue to the " experience " of Christendom, to which he constantly appealed : Mr. Streeter that his historical investigations were bad as historical investigations. I tried to show them all that they were worshipping an idol, or rather propitiating a bogy—that of the Modern Man with his Modern Mind. But the side of the question which is most relevant here is the chapter

on Authority and Experience which I wrote in answer
to Mr. Rawlinson.

According to Mr. Rawlinson, Church authority
consisted of the " collective witness " of Christendom : the fact that people did, in various ages, and
places, find their spiritual needs met by this doctrine
and that was a definite datum for scientific research ;
by inference from such data as this you could infer the
truth of the doctrines in question. (I hope I am not
misrepresenting him : what I have written sounds
more like Tyrrell's point of view, which he certainly
does not share. But I think his use of the word " experience " leads the reader to suppose that experience
is in theology what experiment is in natural science.)
My criticism of this was purely destructive, but it was
not captious ; the argument did profoundly dissatisfy
me. I felt that on such grounds I could never call
myself a Christian ; my own " experience " of Christianity might, for all I knew, be an illusion—how
much more the alleged "experience " of other people ?
I have seldom been more pleased with a compliment
than when the *Daily News* told me I was a sceptic by
nature and by grace a Catholic. " Authority " must
mean more than the results of a scientific induction ;
it must be something *sui generis*, with a corresponding
faculty (of faith), equally *sui generis*, to apprehend its
deliveries.

I am not concerned to argue the point here, as long
as I can make it plain ; but what I naturally ask myself is—How could I talk so boldly about the authority
of the Church without giving some attention to the

question of its source and of its mouthpiece? I think the answer is not really difficult. I was writing an *ad hominem* argument to Anglicans, and I had the formularies of Anglicanism to appeal to, which are, so far as they go, sufficiently definite. But beyond that, I was concerned with writers who professed to reverence tradition, who quoted the Fathers as if they had a right to a respectful hearing ; I was dealing with a public which accepted, nominally at least, the traditions of the Church as the Anglican divines would have accepted them, differing from the Anglican divines only as to the proper limits of the interpretation and "restatement" to which those traditions could properly be subjected. I was thus, I think, within my rights when I suggested to the ordinary layman (whom I had nicknamed "Jones" for the occasion) that he could trust his common-sense to tell him what Christian tradition was.

My reviewers in the secular press were kind beyond anything I could have deserved or expected. The religious organs were mostly so carried away with the desire to pulverize my views that they gave the book a welcome advertisement.[1] The most favourable comment of all came from Catholic papers, which were generous enough to welcome my efforts in defence of tradition without trying to score off me for not being a Catholic myself. Why unfriendly critics told me I ought to be a Roman Catholic I could not and still cannot understand ; the plainest intimation of this kind which I got arose out of a passage in which I

---

[1] I think something over 4000 were sold

had pointed out that the corporal Ascension of our Saviour was unmistakably asserted by the Thirty-nine Articles !

More interesting than the reviews were the letters I received in the course of that autumn and winter. Presbyterians wrote to rebuke me for my obscurantism, ordinary Anglicans to congratulate me on my attitude, some from a quite Protestant standpoint ; clergymen of my own school welcomed me, even Catholics thanked me for bearing witness to some of their principles. I am afraid that I could not answer all these letters, and confined my replies chiefly to those which definitely asked questions. One contribution of the latter description consisted of eight foolscap pages from Father Vassall-Phillips. I had been bold enough to talk, as an Anglican, about the authority of the Church,

nec talia passus Ulixes ;

agreeing with me warmly on various points, he wondered exactly how it was that, in talking of religious "experience," I could say that I would be prepared to doubt the grace of all the Sacraments I had ever received, if I were not *a priori* convinced that they had validity ? Whence, he could not help asking himself, did my *a priori* conviction spring ?

I do not know precisely what answer I made ; I had not intended to evoke criticism from this quarter, and did not feel that the logical coherence of *Some Loose Stones* depended on the link in question. I think, however, that it would be well to give here some indication of the line I used to take at this time when strangers wrote to me (as occasionally happened) or friends consulted me about what Anglicans call " Roman difficulties."

I think I never failed to urge that it was imperative to follow conscience honestly, not to go on drugging it with controversial literature. But I suggested to other people as a duty what I held to be a duty myself —namely, to remain in communion with the Church of England and to work and pray for a final corporate " reunion " with the Holy See. To show that such a reunion was not impossible, I recommended the reading of my old friend *John Inglesant.* If, as that book suggested, there was a time when Roman Catholics could hope to regain the Church of England *en bloc* by reconciling the King ; if a Jesuit could advise the hero to remain an Anglican with this end in view ; if the hero himself could go about the world not quite certain whether he was an Anglican or a Roman Catholic— why should it not be so to-day ? Might it not be that the Church of Rome, disillusioned by failure and embittered by persecution, had lost faith in what was really God's plan for the reconversion of England ?

It hardly needs to be said that the argument is not cogent, simply because, if John Shorthouse was right about Santa Clara's views, it does not follow that Santa Clara (or even the Church of his day) was right in holding them : the Church of Rome has, in any case, had leisure to reconsider her opinion, and my appeal was really from a Pope better informed to a Pope worse informed. However, my business is not with polemics. I think it will be admitted that by this time I was what people are pleased to call " a Roman Catholic in the Church of England." I did not pay much attention to indulgences, though I did not doubt them, but this was the only department of the " modern Roman " devotional system which I did not treasure. I believed that the authority of an infallible Church was necessary to the confident preaching of any Christian doctrine. I believed that the Church of England had no future but in reunion. And yet I had no intention of becoming a Catholic. Since my conversion, people have said to me, " Of course we knew you were on the way to becoming a Catholic." To which (humanly speaking) I have a quite simple reply " I wasn't."

X

THE YEAR OF PAMPHLETS

Constitit, et lacrimans " Quis jam locus" inquit "Achate,
Quae regio in terris nostri non plena laboris?"

ALTHOUGH (I need hardly say) it was not I who
set the fashion, it remains true that I was well
ahead of the market when I published *Naboth's Vineyard* as a tract. For this year—I mean the summer of
1913 to the summer of 1914—was one of almost in-
cessant religious controversy ; the canons boomed
daily against one another in the columns of the *Times*,
missionary meetings were distended to an unwonted
size by the inspiriting effect of a " crisis in the Church ";
Anglican principles were freely discussed in railway
carriages and in Senior Common-rooms, and a friend
of mine was told at Parker's (the Tractarian book-
seller of Oxford) that there had never been such a
demand for religious pamphlets in the last forty
years. There were giants in the field in those days,
and I cannot say of the developments in question
quorum pars magna fui ; but at least *et nos aliquod
nomenque decusque gessimus*—both *Naboth's Vineyard*
and *Some Loose Stones* achieved popularity from the
situation which sprang up after them and quite inde-
pendently of them, and my next literary production

became, by force of bitter circumstances, the epilogue to the controversy.

It is necessary to recall the facts that were then common knowledge, since buried, not by distance of time, but by the obliterating effect of a world war. Representatives of the two Anglican dioceses of Uganda and Mombasa took part that summer in a conference at Kikuyu with representatives of various Free Church missions at which problems of co-operation between the various denominations were discussed. A programme was drawn up (subject, of course, to revision by the home authorities) which recognised among other things the "exchange of pulpits" and the admission of non-Anglicans to Communion in Anglican churches. Both the two dioceses involved belonged to the Church Missionary Society, which is evangelical both in its traditions and in its modern atmosphere. But the neighbouring diocese of Zanzibar belonged to the Universities' Mission to Central Africa, founded under Tractarian influence and supported principally by "advanced" churches in England. Naturally this attitude towards the Free Churches could not commend itself to such a diocese, and the situation that arose was a complicated one— if the Kikuyu resolutions were carried into effect, Anglicans on one side of a quite artificial boundary would be encouraged to communicate at non-episcopal churches, while Anglicans on the other side of it would be forbidden to enter them. There is a "floating population" even in East Africa, and it seemed as if the emigrant from Zanzibar to Mombasa or vice versa would have some difficulty in seeing the point.

There was thus a quite practical difficulty, but the Kikuyu Conference went further. It closed with a United Communion Service conducted by an Anglican bishop in a non-episcopal church, at which Anglicans and non-Anglicans worshipped and communicated together. This was not altogether a unique occurrence : the revisers of the Bible, for example, communicated together at Westminster Abbey. But the circumstances of the occurrence were exceptional, and Bishop Weston, of Zanzibar, felt it his duty to protest. This was not the only symptom which disturbed him. As an accomplished theologian of orthodox tendencies he had read *Foundations*, and seen more clearly than most people the great departures from orthodox tradition which the book involved—particularly in the matter of the Resurrection. Finally, as one jealous for the honour of the Mother of God, he resented the action of the Bishop of St. Albans against the Catholic league, described in the last chapter. He therefore addressed an open letter to the Bishop of St. Albans, really directed *Urbi et Orbi*, in which he protested against all these three devolopments, and followed it up by demanding of the Archbishop of Canterbury (as standing in a peculiar relation to the missionary dioceses) that he should convoke a court to pronounce upon the " heretical " proceedings at Kikuyu.

The Corringham incident, where the Evangelicals appeared as persecutors and their opponents as the victims, was conveniently forgotten : the whole British public and the whole British press fell to wrangling about the other two points. On the matter of intercommunion, the Dean of Durham was the protaganist of Protestantism ; on the question of doctrinal orthodoxy it was Professor Sanday who chiefly espoused the Foundationist cause ; Bishop Weston's most important champion in England was reputed to be the Bishop of Oxford, though he did not greatly involve himself in any newspaper correspondence. The British public, warm-hearted as usual rather than clear-headed, could only see one side to the whole question ; persecution of anybody by anybody about anything must be wrong, and when the offence alleged was one of " charity " towards members of another denomination, the issue became even clearer.. In Oxford itself the academic world of the Senior Common-rooms, which always reflects faithfully the tendencies of the uneducated public, was almost entirely on the side of free speculation about the faith (for there was talk of inhibiting Mr. Streeter) and of "hospitality " to Nonconformists at Anglican altars.

In fact, nothing was wanting to produce a Church crisis, of the magnitude of the " Jerusalem Bishopric," the Colenso schism, and all the excitements of Tractarian days. Now, it is a curious thing about these crises that, nowadays, they always occasion the rumour and sometimes the threat that a large body of orthodox people may be expected to " secede," and yet very few people ever do. The curate hurries to and fro, pale-faced and calling for action, but his

M

vicar, inured to scandals in the establishment, shows no intention of budging.

Satis una superque
Vidimus excidia, et captae superavimus urbi :
Sic, o sic positum affati discedite corpus.

Even I and my friends could remember the "United Communion" at Hereford on the occasion of the Coronation ; we had survived the "Brighton row" and the loss of Caldey, and, while we were all prepared to support Bishop Weston, we made no motion of packing up our trunks.

I found myself, however, at the age of twenty-five, affected by the influence of people younger than myself. I went that winter to San Remo, with two friends who were in search of rest and health—one of these was B, whom I have referred to above. C was writing to one or other of us as frequently as the nature of the Italian postal service would allow. And both of them, neophytes so far as "my religion" was concerned, plainly took the Kikuyu business more seriously than I did. My only way of soothing them was to suggest that the whole battle had not yet been fought ; it was bound to come to a head in 1918, when the next Pan-Anglican Congress would meet : till then we must keep our powder dry. I did very seriously anticipate that the effects of these troubles might be to split the Church of England ; and if this was to be so I wanted to be in at the funeral. Meanwhile, I set about writing an article on the whole question which afterwards appeared in the *British*

Review, and I also prepared a paper about it which I read in Keble the next term.

I do not think that San Remo had much to say to my religious development. We used to hear Benediction there at a convent chapel more exquisitely rendered than I have ever heard it elsewhere, but I was by now sufficiently used to Catholic services not to feel an outsider when I attended them. Not that I ever did on the Continent what I have heard defended as a permissible practice—take Communion from and even confess myself to Catholic priests, who would not realize what I was. The fact that certain priests have been found so ignorant or so wanting in theological principle as to communicate Anglicans deliberately— so one is told—never seemed to me to provide the smallest excuse for presenting oneself, without ex- planation, for Communion in circumstances where one would naturally be mistaken for a Catholic. The fact that I believed myself to be a Catholic made no difference : I was not going to practise deception—a kind of deception which is fortunately very rare. Nor, conversely, did I agree with that strict school of thought which holds that Anglican chaplaincies in Catholic countries are an abomination : propaganda in Catholic countries was obviously wicked, but to supply the religious needs of Europe residents was natural enough. I celebrated at the chaplaincy every Sunday, and on Christmas Day in the presence of a large and startled congregation : " Thank God, *that's* over," a gentleman observed audibly as I came down from the altar, unconsciously giving the response to my Last Gospel. On Christmas Day I also preached, condemning all ideas of " peace on earth " which rested on confusions of thought in the manner of Kikuyu.

Bishop Weston came back to England in 1914, to prefer his charges in person. He visited Oxford and had dinner in my rooms (he is himself a Trinity man) ; a small collection of sympathetic college chaplains came to meet him and discuss things. He pointed out to us that it was a far more awkward situation for us than for himself ; he was master in his own diocese, and commanded the support of the other Universities' Mission bishops, and the sympathy of the whole synod of South Africa : if the worst came to the worst he could defy the people at home. In effect, it will be remembered, the Archbishop decided that no competent court was to be found, and referred the whole dispute to an unofficial commission recently constituted. It seemed probable, especially in view of what happened that summer, that the question would be shelved almost indefinitely—what else were commissions appointed for ? It was a false calculation.

From the Lent of 1914 to the Easter of 1915 I was more fully engaged than ever in preaching and in lecturing. During that Lent, for example, I paid a visit to St. David's College, Lampeter, to put my own point of view before the students ; and so far were the officials of the college from resenting my firebrand activities that Dr. Bebb, the then principal, was kind enough to afford me the hospitality of his own house. I also gave a course of addresses at a church in Worcester under the auspices of the local English Church

Union, under the titles " Two Views of the Church,"
" Two Views of the Faith," " Two Views of the Mass,"
etc. My object was to prove that if you were prepared
to accept views less definite than my own, then you
were logically reduced to taking a " Kikuyu " view of
the Church, a *Foundations* view of the Faith, and so
on. In fact, my efforts were directed not so much to
convincing those who held a merely " Liberal " standpoint about ecclesiastical definitions, as to rallying
cautious, yet orthodox " High Churchmen " to the
standard of sacramentalism. In Holy Week I went
down to Plymouth, having obtained leave from the
Bishop to preach a series of non-controversial addresses
on the Passion, including the devotion of the Three
Hours, at St. James's.

It was in an interval of these activities that I went to
stay at Cranborne for a reading party. I think I did
most of the work, for my sermons kept me hard at it.
But now and then, when I was waiting for the finish of
an unnecessarily protracted game of billiards, I would
prowl round the shelves that lined the walls of the
library there, and so came to renew my acquaintance
with the admirable satirical vein of Dean Swift. It
was in a railway carriage that the idea occurred to me
of utilizing his manner for the conveyance of an
ecclesiastical message. The idea slept in my mind,
and the very moment I had returned from preaching
the Three Hours it claimed me imperiously. The old
atmosphere of August, 1913, was round me ; Mr. Child
and Mr. Baker were still there, though on this occasion
I was staying with Mr. Miers, the vicar ; B was with

me, and Mr. Gurney suddenly arrived from Cologne, where he had meant to spend Holy Week, complaining that they did not " do things properly " at the Cathedral there. I wrote feverishly, as if my hands from their long practice could not be kept off the keys of my typewriter : the result was ready by Easter Tuesday. Thus, whereas *Absolute and Abitophell* was the work of months, *Reunion All Round* (for so I had labelled my new pasquinade) was all completed in four days. Completed, that is, as far as writing went, for the production was a matter of anxious care both to Mr. Gurney and to myself ; the type and the spelling of Swift's day had to be carefully imitated, as well as the rubrication of the title-page : even the paper was of a brownish cream colour, that gave the impression of having been soiled by age. I dedicated the book to Mr. and Mrs. Henry Head, friends whom I had met with Mr. Lyon at Middlecot, and discovered to be devoted admirers of Swift.

The argument of the book was a simple *reductio ad absurdum*. If (as the British public seemed to think) it was the duty of all *Christian* bodies to unite for worship, sinking their differences on each side, why should the movement be confined to Christians ? What about the Jews, from whom we were only separated by the Council of Jerusalem ? And if the Jews, why not the Mohammedans ? We could always split the difference between monogamy and tetragamy by having two wives all round. The Brahmins presented few difficulties : the worshippers of Mumbo-jumbo only needed a passing reference. At this point the

spirit of satire carried me away, and I suggested with
every appearance of misgiving that perhaps after all,
given proper precautions, charity should demand of
us that we should accept the submission of the Pope.
After making arrangements for the suitable degrada-
tion of the Roman hierarchy, I went boldly forward to
the case of the atheists, and suggested that we might
join with them in a common definition of the Divine
Nature, which should assert it to be such as to involve
Existence and Non-existence simultaneously.   Here,
with a few exhortations to the public, I left my argument to my readers.

Now, a *reductio ad absurdum* argument may be used
merely for fun, and without any serious purpose of
satire behind it.   But I did not write in this vein of
good-tempered exaggeration :   I meant what I said—
or rather, of course, I meant the opposite of what I
said.   If you are to do this, your logical developments
must depend upon a valid reasoning process—in
satire, no less than in a mathematical treatise.   Thus,
although it was possible to regard *Reunion All Round*
as merely a graceful *jeu d'esprit*, I meant it for much
more than this :   I meant that, if the principles of
Kikuyu were right, something like this (discounting,
of course, the casual absurdities) did really follow as a
logical consequence.   If, in the name of charity, it was
the duty of the Church to aim at the inclusion of all
good men who were professing Christians, and herself
make sacrifices in order to do so, why should she not
have the same duty in connection with all good men
simply because they were good ?   Why should a belief,

often of the shadowiest, in the undefined " Divinity " of Christ be a touchstone of Church membership ? For the life of me I could never see why we had to regret being out of communion with a good man like Dr. Horton, more than being out of communion with a good man like Professor Gilbert Murray, who repudiates Theism. If the Church, without being called "uncharitable," is to have tests and definitions at all, why should you draw the line at this test or that definition, and cry out in horror, " No, no, that would be uncharitable ? "

I know that some of my Anglican readers think all this very preposterous ; but we must wait till Theosophy has come out a little more into the light of day. I have read a manual of theosophical belief which declares confidently that the religion of the future lies in a combination of all that is best in Christianity and Brahminism—that very combination that tickled us so when we read it in *Reunion All Round*. And Mr. Wells, who is an adept at the logical carrying out of implied principles, has already provided us with a religion in which a personal God, not an Incarnate God, is asserted as a basis of doctrine.

Once again the secular press was more kind to me than the ecclesiastical, and the advertisement of the book in the S.S.P.P. catalogue still, I think, contains the following press comment :

" The turn of Swift's sentences is admirably caught."
Spectator.
"A foolish, flippant skit."
Cambridge Christian Life.

But the book enjoyed a wider popularity than its press notices might have warranted ; it was short, readable, and eminently topical. If reports were true, it was read by a community of Catholic nuns, who supposed the suggestions to be quite serious ; it was read in refectory at the English College, under the impression that I was a Catholic, and caused great doubts of my salvation when it proved that I was not ; it was read to the Prime Minister as he sat in bathing costume on the river-bank in that hottest of summers. I was even told that it gained the hearts of the episcopate, chiefly owing to an undesigned allusion in the sub-title—but stay, even the Anglican episcopate has its secrets. It won, in cold print, the commendation of my earliest master and model, Mr. G. K. Chesterton.

During this year I increased my circle of Catholic friends. I had enjoyed already the hospitality of Father Lang while he was chaplain at Oxford, but his successor, Father Maturin, was a man with whom (in spite of the obvious sanctity of his life) I felt an unusual degree of human contact. By origin he was one of my own Cowley Fathers ; in the controversies of the moment he took an interest which hardly pretended to be dispassionate. From his surprise at the calmness with which the Kikuyu incident was regarded you might have thought him an Anglican still. I was always rather afraid of Catholic priests at this time, feeling that they might be " getting at me," but Father Maturin always treated you with the openness of a friend. I made another acquaintance, slight at the time, but destined to develop, with the Catholic priest-

hood when, at one of Miss Anderson's "evenings" at
4 Broad Street, I met the friend of more than one of
my friends, Father Martindale. Mr. and Mrs. Wilfrid
Ward paid a visit to Oxford, and I met them both at
Mr. Urquhart's table and at Mr. Raper's ; Mrs. Ward
took me to task over a heresy in *Some Loose Stones*,
which I afterwards tried to defend in the preface to
the second edition ; I freely admit that she has St.
Thomas on her side, and I have no doubt that she is
right, but I was pleased to be able to quote St. Leo in
contradiction of her. To Mr. Urquhart also I owed the
privilege of sitting at the same table with the Cardinal
Archbishop. I did not, however, like some of my
school, make a point of meeting Catholics and exchang-
ing views with them ; their existence in the abstract I
welcomed, and felt every set-back to Catholicism as a
personal loss, but in the presence of Catholics, except
my old friends, I seldom failed to feel uneasy.

In the summer vacation I was at work again. Messrs.
Longmans had suggested an orthodox substitute for
Foundations. For various reasons this work, which
was to be of joint authorship, never saw the light, at
least in the form contemplated ; but all July I was
with Mr. Williams, first at Brighton and then at Plymouth, alternately hammering at my own subject
(the Incarnation) and debating with him acrimoniously
on the views he meant to express about authority. To
me an authority which could not be traced back to the
mediæval Roman Church, without admixture of
Eastern Orthodoxy, was still impossible. From
Brighton I fulfilled a preaching engagement which

made me feel that my recent writings had given me a
standing even in prudent Anglo-Catholic circles—I
delivered the sermon at the annual festival of the
St. Margaret's Sisterhood, East Grinstead, where the
most unimpeachable bulwarks of the Tractarian tradition are liable to appear.   An address to the Oxford
E.C.U. about the need of an authority which could say
to the unorthodox theologian not merely " Resign ! "
but " Recant ! "—I did not, of course, suggest thumb-
screws or faggots, but merely a voice speaking with the
certainty of divine guidance—was published about
this time, and commended me afresh to my old Mentor,
Mr. Coles. I no longer felt myself an Ishmael and an
outlaw. Another of my closest friends at Oxford had
begun to make his confessions ; yet another had (so
to speak) put himself under instruction, and I looked
forward with bright hopes to a reading party in
August.

History will revere the name of one of our present
statesmen, whose *obiter dictum* used often to be quoted,
" I never read the papers." I never read the papers at
this time, and it was only in casual conversation I
learned that all was not well with Europe.   Then the
bugles went round to call up the Naval Reserve ; a
big German cargo ship sulkily submitted to be towed
across the Sound into its long resting-place, and as I
travelled north to stay with B in the Midlands, I read
the Foreign Secretary's speech.

XI

CARRYING ON

Nil super imperio moveor ; speravimus ista
Dum fortuna fuit.

I HAD arranged to have a reading party with several
of my undergraduate friends at More Hall, near
Stroud. It is a beautiful country house, the centre of a
religious community and an admirable place for retreats ; the kindness of Father Sharpe had put it at
my disposal for use during the last three weeks of
August, for this unmonastic purpose. It will readily
be conceived that by the tenth of August the undergraduate members of the party were all at the disposal
of Lord Kitchener, and I found myself, as it were,
forced into a retreat. In those days of overpowering
depression and nightmare anticipations, when first the
London Gazette and then the casualty lists began to
fill with familiar names, and when the scenes that to
me were all holy ground fell one by one into the power
of the invader, I lived in complete solitude (apart from
the presence of a lay brother who looked after my
wants) corresponding with my friends and devoting
my prayers on their behalf. About six hours of the day
I spent over my devotions ; for the rest I was writing
or taking long, lonely walks through the path-ridden
woods that crown those admirable hills.

It is extraordinary to me to reflect that this was the only formal retreat I made between my Anglican ordination and my conversion. I may perhaps have given the impression that my friends and I spent our time in perpetual holiday; the inference would be quite unjust : and even when I was on holiday at Plymouth (for example) each of us would be " saying his Mass " daily and otherwise observing the ordinary behaviour of a (secular) Catholic priest. Meditation, too, I practised as a matter of course, though at times (partly through circumstances) irregularly, having indeed far more aptitude for mental than for vocal prayer. But when I wanted to go into retreat, none were advertised; when retreats were advertised, I could not go ; and somehow I lacked the initiative to make a solitary retreat until it was thus forced upon me. I had a chapel where I could celebrate daily, with the Blessed Sacrament reserved, and, so far as the terrors and distractions of the time allowed, I found in my hermit existence an extraordinary peace. I passed the whole three weeks in this way.

One of my friends told me afterwards that he had imagined my retreat (to which I sacrificed several rival attractions) to be a sign of uneasiness about the " Roman question." As a matter of fact, even when I was interrogating my conscience most strictly, I was wholly without qualm of this kind ; I turned to my own religion for spiritual comfort and, however little progress I may have made, never once found it shallow or unsatisfactory. I went to the Catholic Church at Stroud when the Sacrament was exposed there, merely because there was exposition : I had no doubt of my own sacraments.

Another question did, of course, present itself to me ; and probably (through a foreshortening of historical perspective) presents itself even more readily to the reader : what was my attitude towards military service ? It is singularly illustrative of the positiveness of my then conditions. Later (as is well known) the Bishops decided against the adoption of a combatant status by the clergy, and their view was ratified by the Government when service became compulsory. Some of the Bishops appealed to Catholic precedent ; others with no less effect to Protestant traditions : the Reformers generally recognized the unsuitability for a minister of the profession of arms, and readers of Macaulay's history will remember the horror he expresses in speaking of Bishop Walker, hero of the siege of Derry, who after the siege put himself in the position of a combatant. I did not wait for a moment upon episcopal decisions ; I turned up St. Thomas immediately, discovered that the profession of arms was forbidden to the clergy except (as in France) under coercion, and had no hesitation at all about my attitude. St. Thomas represented the Western Church, the Church to which I owed allegiance.

In parenthesis I may say that I was not proof against the desire to find some appropriate form of usefulness. It was on the feast of St. Raymund Nonnatus, while I was reading the description in the second nocturn of his ideal of voluntary captivity, that I suddenly became impressed with the spiritual lot of those " Church of England" soldiers who would fall into enemy hands. An encyclopædia told me that 300,000 Frenchmen were prisoners in Germany in 1871 : they were at least cared for by priests of their own religion. But Anglicans— and there might well be some convinced Anglicans among them, considering the numerous daily accessions to our fighting forces—would be cut off from the ministrations of the Rhineland clergy, yet would derive little satisfaction from such visits as the " grim Geneva ministers " might pay them. I wrote at once to the Bishop of London, suggesting that the German Government might be induced to allow a few Anglican priests to share the captivity of our soldiers, living under internment conditions and ranking as prisoners. The Bishop of London turned me over to Bishop Bury, of " Northern and Central Europe," who was very kind in agitating on my behalf (naturally I had offered myself for the scheme), and it went to the Foreign Office : they decided that it would not be proper for the British Government to put itself under any obligation to an enemy power. Later, in 1916, the scheme was revived, but I was by that time too far gone in uncertainty to avail myself of the chance : I do not know what became of it, but I never heard of any actual result.

It is as well to say here that, although I had the opportunity of securing myself a chaplaincy by devious ways, I held back owing to the pronouncedly anti-Sacramentalist attitude which then almost entirely dominated, and still largely dominates, the Chaplains' Department and many of the senior chaplains. My behaviour, I felt, would involve me in Field Punishment No. 1 long before I reached the scene of active operations.

I had, as it proved, something positive to show for my time at More Hall. I used to pray for an hour each day on behalf of the various participants in and sufferers through the war, dividing them up (for I cannot get on without headings) into various categories. It occurred to me after a time to form out of these, a scheme of intercession which might be useful to others : by way of giving it colour, I designed the scheme so as to include twelve divisions of five minutes each, and sent the whole to the Society of SS. Peter and Paul with the suggestion that each division should have a picture of a clock in front of it, the hands arranged appropriately for the various intervals. Whether this publicist's stratagem, or some usefulness in the prayers themselves, or the fact that half the profits were devoted to the Prince of Wales's Fund, was the recommendation of the book, I do not know : but *An Hour at the Front* (so we called it) sold something over 70,000 copies, mostly in the first month or two after its appearance. It was meant, of course, for people at home, but I have heard of its being used in the trenches. Except for the doctrine of Merit, on which I naturally insisted, it was far from being a controversial production ; in spite of (or because of) this it seemed to have a considerable vogue amongst Catholics.

At the beginning of September I went to Ludlow, where I was to read a paper before the local branch of the English Church Union. The same paper was subsequently read to a gathering, including all shades of clerical opinion, at Birmingham. I do not know which of the two audiences was more obviously mystified or (probably) more profoundly shocked. I published the paper afterwards anonymously, as one of the " York books " produced by the Society of SS. Peter and Paul, under the title *Between Two Extremes*. My purpose was to show that it was possible for people like myself to claim every liberty in the way of " Romanizing " without lending thereby any sanction or countenance to the " Liberal " clergymen who, like ourselves, were accused of disloyalty to the Church of England. For (I argued) the Church of England did as a matter of history make every reasonable concession in order to include within her borders the Puritans, who had too little belief in supernatural religion ; it made no effort whatever to include the Roman Catholics, who believed too much. Thus all Anglican formularies were conceived as a minimum of belief ; no clear attempt had been made to define the maximum. The disloyalty of believing less than the fixed minimum was patent, but if anybody said to us, " You are exceeding the maximum," we had a right to inquire how he knew. This point of view I still think historically sound so far as the later revisions of the Prayer Book are concerned—I mean, that it was always the minimizers and not the maximizers who were being considered. Nor can I accuse myself of paradox for having suggested that there was nothing in Anglican formularies which either deliberately

N

forbade the Reservation of the Sacrament, or explicitly made Confession optional rather than obligatory : the effort to establish the contrary by reference to Prayer Book rubrics which were not designed to meet the case has always seemed to me mere special pleading. I do not know that the tract aroused much attention, but I believe Lord Halifax recommended it at a general meeting of the English Church Union.

I think I ought to say here that, often as I tried to convince people of the inconsistency between Modernist theology and the fundamental principles of Anglicanism, at no time did I urge, or indeed think desirable, the ejection of Modernists from their benefices, still less from the Church itself. This was not because I disapproved in the abstract of strict disciplinary action, but because in my view (according to which there was no living authority in the Anglican Church) there was no machinery which could justifiably persecute either the Modernists or ourselves. I once even constructed, in a half-serious moment, a teleological explanation of the existence of the Anglican Communion. Providence, in allowing for the necessary rise and growth of heresies in the eighteenth and nineteenth centuries, applied a sort of tourniquet to one arm of the Church (the arm is the Church of England), so as to stop the free circulation of the blood between it and the main body—thus the arm could be infected with the poison of Modernism, and the virus could be allowed to work itself out there. When the virus had worked itself out, it would be time for the removal of the tourniquet, i.e. for the reconciliation of the Anglican Communion. I do not know if the allegory is medically accurate ; theologically it is at least ingenious.

As far as I can remember, I incorporated in *Between Two Extremes* parts of an address which I gave soon afterwards to a meeting of clergymen at Durham. It was on the old subject of authority and Liberalism, but quotation from it is not necessary here, for it did nothing to advance my position. I had demurred somewhat to fulfilling this engagement, because I felt it as something of an indecency that we should still be squabbling while our country was in arms. During all this early part of the war I pleaded for a sort of *union sacrée*—we should abstain from controversy, and expect our opponents to do the same : and I tried as far as possible to refrain from destructive criticism and agitation. The fact that I allowed a second edition of *Some Loose Stones* to appear was only due to a technical necessity in the matter of printing.

On the other hand, I did firmly maintain that this was the time for introducing such devotional developments as would make for the consolation of the afflicted and the kindling of our countrymen's waning enthusiasm for religion. I refer, in particular, of course, to the Reservation of the Blessed Sacrament. It could not be thought underhand to consolidate our own position, for

Belli commercia Turnus
Sustulit ista prior—

the Evangelicals were already consolidating theirs,
and were making a strong " bid " for the influencing
of our fighting forces. In that November (of 1914) I
organized (for there seemed to be no one else to organize
it) an adaptation of the Forty Hours' Exposition in
various English towns. True to the tradition of our
military censorship, I will not name the towns :
suffice it to say that they were widely distributed, and
that no town had the " Exposition " in progress for
more than a single period of two days. Sundays had
to be omitted, owing to practical difficulties, but on
any week-day in that November it was possible to
reflect that at one town in England the Blessed Sacrament was being adored. The precise circumstances
(e.g. the use or non-use of the Monstrance) were left
to individual tastes ; the form for the Masses of
Exposition and Reposition was specially printed and
circulated.

The Reservation of the Sacrament in public had, of
course, by then, and has since, grown enormously.
As I mentioned above, there was a time when only
half a dozen London churches practised Reservation ;
their present number it would be dangerous to in-
vestigate and wearisome to count. The movement in
the provinces is parallel, though always somewhat
behindhand. Nor is it fair to accuse the priests who
have made this innovation during the war of seizing
upon a time of public distraction in order to escape
observation : the fact is that, in the effort to keep up
the standard of intercession at a time when it was
badly needed, they felt they could not deny their con-

gregations any possible help to devotion. For myself and my friends, the only wonder was that the discovery was not made earlier ; one of us, being congratulated on the installation of a tabernacle by his vicar, replied grimly, " Yes, but it took the blood of nine nations to do it."

I did, however, have one more opportunity of elucidating in public my ideas about authority. Mr. Underhill, of St. Alban's, Birmingham, invited Mr. Williams and myself to address a meeting of priests from Birmingham and its neighbourhood on that subject. Dr. Darwell Stone was to sum up and make final criticisms on the situation. To a certain extent, Mr. Williams and I managed to partition our subject beforehand, so that our speeches should be complementary rather than contradictory; they could not be actually consistent. Generally speaking, the position I supported was as follows : That since the Reformation caused no real breach of " continuity," everything that was binding on the English Church in 1500 was binding on it still, in the same measure, except in so far as certain modifications introduced by secular law had made it natural (though not objectively justifiable) for Englishmen to neglect certain obligations that were previously recognized, such as that of Confession at Easter. Our object was to persuade Englishmen to undertake voluntarily the obligations from which, in secular law, they were dispensed. (I suppose that the obligation of Friday abstinence is still on the Statute Book.) As for the regulations which the Church of Rome had seen fit to make since the Reformation, they were not in strictness obligatory (else were our faith vain) but they were laudable practices: and if a plain question arose " Does my duty lie this way, or that ? " the course prescribed by the Church of Rome had a sort of contingent or congruous authority which it would be temerarious to overlook. Thus, if in one year the Feast of the Immaculate Conception was of obligation for Roman Catholics, and the next year a feast of devotion, it would be disloyal in Anglicans to pretermit attendance at Mass in the former year, though not actually mortal sin. Mr. Williams, of course, took an entirely different line, which, though less satisfactory to the Papalizing instinct, was probably more reasonable from a general point of view.

This was still in the autumn of 1914. Meanwhile, it need hardly be said, Oxford had become a shadow of its former self. In the summer term I had six undergraduate friends who regularly served me at the altar ; in the Michaelmas term all were far off and in uniform. Trinity was already reduced to a third of its normal size. My chief object was to keep in touch with my friends, and to keep them in touch with one another— this was in the days when a six months' war seemed possible ; I spent much of my time writing letters, entertained freely when undergraduates came up for the night or for the week-end, and in my vacations lost no opportunity of paying visits. Between September, 1914, and May, 1915, I had visited friends at Aldershot (twice), Camberley, Frensham, Churn, Grantham, Wendover, High Wycombe, Southend, Folkestone, and

Bournemouth, apart from numerous meetings both in Oxford and London.

Three deaths of Catholics during these first few months of the war made an especial impression on me. The late Holy Father was the subject of a bitter attack in one of the Anglican Church newspapers, an attack which maddened me, as I am glad to say it disgusted most people, by its virulent abuse of a great Prelate whose relics had hardly yet been committed to the grave. Monsignor Benson I had only met once, but I never felt towards him that irritation which his name often aroused among my friends, and I always looked on him as the guide who had led me to Catholic truth—I did not know then that he used to pray for my conversion. I celebrated, that All Souls' Day, at an Anglican sisterhood, and began the service by asking prayers especially for a list of names, including those of " Pius, Bishop of Rome, and Robert Hugh Benson, priest."

Father Maturin's death was more personal to me, as well as more impressive from the horror of its circumstances. It was easy to conjure up the picture of him, as he moved fearlessly to and fro in those last moments on the *Lusitania*. If ever anything should go wrong, I felt, here was one friend the less to welcome me on the other side.

Non licuit fines Italos, fataliaque arva,
Nec tecum Ansonium, quicumque est, quaerere Thybrim :

I was to miss one voice of congratulation, when I too had to pay the Price of Unity.

The question of the Roman claims was forced upon my notice during the winter of 1914–1915. An old Eton and Oxford friend wrote to me and explained that he was in difficulties about them. I replied at some length, as I was accustomed to write in such cases, explaining my view of our mission as Anglicans, but with this proviso—that he was going out to face the risk of sudden death, and I was not. Consequently, if on examining his conscience he found that he was " not long for " the Church of England, he would be justified in anticipating a later decision and making his submission at once. This side of the question, which had not previously occurred to me, troubled me a little ; and before Christmas I found opportunities to put the same point of view before B and C, who (as I have said) had shown signs of unrest during the Kikuyu debate. The answer was in both cases the same—that they were prepared to face death as they were.

Although the University and Trinity were so depleted in numbers these two terms, the first two terms of the war, were by no means idle for me ; so far as preaching goes, I was at my most active. There is no point in trying to construct a complete list, but some instances may suffice by way of illustration. I preached at York for the first evensong of Michaelmas, at Southampton for the second ; at All Saints', Margaret Street, for their patronal octave, at St. Martin's, Worcester, for theirs. I delivered the annual sermon to university students at St. Giles's, Reading. In the Lent term, at a few hours' notice, I supplied the place of a bishop who was to have given the Sunday evening sermon at the University Church: some Catholic friends who came to hear me noted with delight that as I climbed into Newman's pulpit for the first (and only) time, the congregation was singing a hymn, and it was "Lead, Kindly Light." (I noticed the coincidence myself, but only with amusement.) Before Lent, I was preaching at St. Barnabas's, Oxford, during Lent at St. Martin's, Worcester again (a course), at St. Silas's, Kentish Town, and at Christ Church, South Hackney. I also preached one Sunday morning at Shrewsbury Chapel. In Holy Week, I gave a course of addresses simultaneously (as it were) at St. Mary's, Graham Street, and All Saints', Margaret Street. I mean, it needed a fast taxi to carry me from one church to the other each afternoon. At Graham Street I conducted the devotion of the Three Hours, and preached on Easter Day.

The course of Holy Week addresses was upon the subject of impetrative prayer, and the subjects were (1) the goodness of God (*Abba Pater*), (2) the omnipotence of God (*omnia tibi possibilia*), (3) the propriety of interceding for special and personal objects (*transeat a me calix iste*), (4) acquiescence in the Will of God as the highest form of prayer (*fiat voluntas tua*). My idea was that people were more than ever wanting to pray, yet more than ever being tempted by doubts about the efficacy of prayer: I wanted to state the Catholic doctrine in its fulness, instructing rather than indulging in apologetic. The addresses were published by the Society of SS. Peter and Paul under the title *Bread or*

Stone ? Among various kind notices of the book I may mention a letter from Sir Bertram Windle, who quoted from the book as evidence of the fact that even Protestant writers still believed in the efficacy of intercession.

It need not be said that Oxford had become a somewhat depressing place, at least for one accustomed to spend most of his time with undergraduates. There was a period, I think it was about November, 1914, when I seriously considered the possibility that I ought to leave Oxford and take up some other form of work—so deep a melancholy had settled over my spirits, so ineffective seemed the functions of a college chaplain. But I was not in any despondency about my personal vocation ; on the contrary, it will be seen from my list of preaching engagements that my existence was being recognized, and not only by institutions inspired with my own special point of view ; further, the " theological dinner," a most select circle of Oxford theologians, had done me the honour of electing me to its membership—I was easily the junior member. Nor was I without hopes of my officer friends, and that Easter one of the most intimate of them made his first confession to me, expecting to be ordered abroad shortly. I had still no quarrel with my position as an Anglican, but only with my position as chaplain. Yet several of my friends were emphatic in telling me to " carry on."

A compromise finally suggested itself. When I went down to Shrewsbury towards the end of Lent, I found that several of the junior masters still left were asking

to be released for military service. One of these was
Mr. Southwell, whom I had known in college at Eton
and (a little) at Magdalen. The headmaster seemed
to be in despair at the losses that threatened him ;
he was, I need hardly say, Mr. Alington, whom I have
already mentioned as having been master in college
when I was at school. I owed much to him, and the
school itself has been kind to me. I therefore obtained
from Trinity a special temporary leave of absence, and
offered to go to Shrewsbury and keep Mr. Southwell's place warm for him. The offer was accepted
with a readiness that, even at such a time, was
flattering.

I had two scruples in making this arrangement.
In the first place, from all I knew of parents, I was
inclined to suppose that my teaching of divinity might
make trouble,[1] if any echoes of it reached paternal
breakfast-tables. (Had I been able to gauge beforehand the receptiveness of my form, I could have made
my mind easy on this score.) In the second place, since
Shrewsbury was not well provided with churches of my
own type, and first lesson was first lesson, it seemed
probable that I should have to discontinue my practice
of celebrating as nearly as possible every day. A
modus vivendi presented itself which met both difficulties. I arranged to be free for all week-ends to go

---

[1] Mr. Alington loved to describe the horror with which he read in a
parent's letter, "I hear that my son is being taught by Mr. Knox, of
Trinity, who ——," and his relief at turning the page and reading, "has
done so much to defend the faith," etc.

up to Oxford or London ; since I was not accepting
any salary beyond my keep, I did not feel such an
arrangement unreasonable, and it saved me from the
two divinity lessons as well as giving me the opportunity to celebrate on Sundays and Mondays. Further,
Mr. Alington obtained leave for me from the Bishop
of Lichfield to celebrate on Thursdays in a private
chapel in the School House. I took advice on the
subject from Mr. Howell (of Graham Street), and he
agreed that with such an arrangement my devotional
life need not suffer.

Most of this (Easter) vacation, when I was not with
friends at military centres, I was staying with Mr.
Gurney at Albemarle Street. Just before I went to
Shrewsbury I attended a meeting which stands out
unique in my memory. Some time before, Mr. Mackay
(of Margaret Street) had collected a band of sympathetic incumbents, twelve in all, who should consult
from time to time on matters of Church policy. They
were known as "the twelve Apostles," and their
meetings, I believe, still continue. Fearing that the
unbeneficed clergy might become mutinous at the
reflection that this Provisional Government of their
vicar's was taking counsel over their heads, Mr. Howell
(of Graham Street), himself not the least of the
" Apostles," formed a sort of society of curates, which
he christened " The Band of Hope." On this occasion,
a joint meeting of the two bodies was to be held ; the
subject was the burning question of the adoration of
the Blessed Sacrament, and Mr. Underhill, of Birming-

ham, an incumbent, but curatophil in tendency, was
to open the meeting.

Eight or nine of us (the unbeneficed) filed one by
one, frock-coated, into a private room at Pagani's
(proximity determined the spot) for a preliminary
dinner. I do not think I can remember a more brilliant
occasion ; we were all friends, mostly of an age, and
our community of ecclesiastical thought gave rise, it
must be admitted, to a common sense of humour. It
was easy to say of us at this time that we thought what
we thought, did what we did, for fun. I repudiate the
accusation entirely, but nobody shall persuade me
that it was not fun doing it. The meeting itself was
large and threatened at times to be stormy, but the
admirable tact of Mr. Mackay succeeded in keeping
the peace. I spoke as neither vicar nor curate, strongly
urging the claims of those extremist churches which
would not " toe the line " as laid down by the Apostles
—St. Saviour's, Hoxton, was the instance in everybody's mind.

Miseri, quibus ultimus esset Ille dies, so far at least
as I myself, and my association with these like-minded
friends, was concerned ; I never spoke again in defence
of such a policy.

> We were young, we were merry, we were very, very wise,
>   And the true word was spoken at our feast ;
> But there passed us a woman with the West in her eyes,
>   And a man with his back to the East.

That very day an ominous light-blue brochure had
appeared, containing the report of the Archbishop's
Commission on the questions raised by the Kikuyu

Conference. Our party, the Band of Hope, found it merely a subject for amusement ; our elders, more closely bound to the Tractarian tradition, shook their heads over it and passed resolutions, but we knew that nothing would come of it.

Frankly, the document hedged. It asserted roundly that Anglicans ought not to receive Nonconformist Sacraments, since we were bound to take our stand upon the threefold order of the ministry. With no less definiteness it stated that, where exceptional circumstances arose, it was quite legitimate for Anglican priests to admit members of the Nonconformist bodies to Communion. The third point raised was whether the United Communion Service at Kikuyu was or was not reprehensible. I do not think I was unjust in declaring (at dinner) that on this third point "the Commission comes to the conclusion that the service at Kikuyu was eminently pleasing to God, and must on no account be repeated."

My attitude, as I say, was that of my friends ; the "decision" was not one to be taken seriously. I had indeed at one time felt that the Church of England would be very gravely compromised by any concession on the part of the Archbishop—not because, on my view, the Archbishop spoke with the voice of the Church, or anything like it, but because if even an Archbishop declared himself uncompromisingly, it must serve as a symptom of the fact that Tractarianism was hopelessly in the minority. Indeed, I am assured that in taking a Monday constitutional with Mr.

Williams and Mr. Allen (of Pembroke) round Addison's
Walk (in 1914) I suggested that it would be our duty to
leave the Church of England ; and I can certainly
remember asking Mr. Allen, " Hang it all, what would
you do, then, if the Archbishop decided the wrong
way ? " and his replying, " I should go home and
smoke a pipe." But I cannot but think the situation
I then had in mind was that of the Archbishop, sitting
in a solemnly constituted Court, ratifying judicially
the whole Kikuyu proceeding : not merely issuing a
report by a commission which made no claim to legislative authority. In any case, I must insist that I was
not afraid of any " decision " of the Archbishop's as an
authoritative declaration, but of the state of general
feeling amongst Anglicans which alone would make
such a bold decision possible.

Now, this was not a bold decision. Had it been
made in 1914 it would have been formidable, in spite
of the apologetic tone in which most of it was couched.
But when it came out in this hole-and-corner way,
in war time, with the eyes of Europe turned elsewhere,
and behind the barrage of a world's artillery, it seemed
to me to have lost (if only on that ground) all its force
as a pronouncement. My only complaint was that it
should have been produced at such a moment (especially if, as was publicly stated and not denied at the
time, the findings of the Commission had been in the
Archbishop's pocket for some months). I resented
the appearance of the document at a moment when it
might cause trouble to the consciences of some who
were just going out with Kitchener's First Army.

But for myself I did not give a thought to it, and I went to Shrewsbury as convinced as ever that my mission was to fight heresy and denounce compromise within the Communion of the Church of England.

XII

SEEING A GHOST

Haud aliter puppesque tuae pubesque tuorum
Aut portum tenet, aut pleno subit ostia velo.
Perge modo, et qua te ducit via, dirige gressum.

I THINK it will conduce to the clearness of my narrative if I omit to give at this point any record of my Shrewsbury impressions, deferring that till a later chapter. For, after all, during this first term of my residence there I was going away for practically all my week ends, and the issues that were affecting the current of my life were being decided elsewhere. Nor in those first three months, when I was not certain from the first that I should be able to stay for a second term, had the place gained that grip upon my affections which it afterwards held, and holds.

Mr. Wilfrid Moor, then a curate at Margaret Street, had taken the report of the Archbishop's Commission in a more serious spirit than the rest of us. But then, he had never had his conscience so well in hand as the rest of us, and what seemed straws to us had often threatened to destroy his equilibrium. But when once anybody goes down with " Roman fever," the infection rarely fails to spread itself; *proximus ardet Ucalegon,* and the blaze once kindled is not easily extinguished. As a matter of fact, Mr. Moor hesitated

for several months ; but almost from the first the fire
had communicated itself to a layman, both his friend
and mine. This friend had not our opportunities of
" thinking things over " ; he was just about to take a
commission, and the scandal of Kikuyu (so it appeared
to him) relieved him of the dreaded prospect of en-
rolling himself " C. of E." I wrote to him, in a rather
flippant tone, I am afraid, justifying his action in the
circumstances, but explaining that I personally had
no intention of letting myself be disturbed by the
ineffectual thunders of Lambeth. Almost immediately
afterwards I had a letter from B ; he had been discussing things with the friend in question ; he was
just going up home ; he wanted my advice.

For a long afternoon, sitting over a refractory fire,
we canvassed the subject. For myself, I could only
renew my previous advice to him ; I was content with
my position, but (as I had told him in 1913) I did not
think we had come to the end of it yet. In 1918, if not
earlier, the whole subject would come up afresh, and
might well give rise to some semi-official resolutions,
not judicial, like the present, but legislative in effect,
which it would be hard for the most thick-skinned of
extremists to ignore. I was content to wait—rather,
I felt it my duty to wait, till that came : if things
should go wrong for us, then I hoped I would not be
alone, and would certainly make every effort not to be
alone, in repudiating the Church of England and asking
for admission to what would then be the only possible
church. But what would my feelings be then if he had
been killed in the meantime, still an Anglican through

my inspiration and advice? I told him I could not advise him, except (of course) to follow his conscience ; I suggested further that he might consult C, who, as I have already mentioned, had shared his impatience in the winter of 1913.

I saw C myself soon afterwards. He agreed with B that the Anglican situation had become impossible : he did not, however, urge the same view on me, admitting that it was probably my duty to weigh my actions even if I felt doubtful. In the event, B was received a few days afterwards at Farm Street : C did not find the transition so easy, and, though repudiating our former position, felt that he could not make a further decision until he had time for thought. B went to the Dardanelles in June, C to France in August. In evidence of what my own feelings were, it is sufficient for me to recall that I stumbled at this time, in a collection of sermons, on Newman's last sermon at Littlemore—that on the Parting of Friends ; and the phrase in it which reflected my feelings was that in which he says of David and Jonathan, " O hard destiny, except the All-merciful had so willed it, that such companions might not walk in the House of God as friends ! " Now, at any rate, to be an Anglican meant something of a sacrifice.

It is perfectly open to anyone to say, " Yes, and a sacrifice which you only made, whole-heartedly at least, for about a fortnight." It is not so that I interpreted, or interpret, my feelings : I must leave it at that. What happened was that an impression forced itself on me which might have forced itself on me at

any time in the past five years. Here was I scheming
for the future of Anglicanism, forcing on issues,
revelling in crises, and in what strength ? I was walking on the tight-rope, but all the time with a net under-
neath me—the Roman Catholic Church. If I fell, her
arms were there to catch me ; that is, if I came to feel
bound to leave my present communion, I had a permanent vacancy for me elsewhere. And, when it came
to conversation with a friend who might well be going
out to his death, I found myself saying, " Of course, in
three years' time I may not be an Anglican myself."
What sort of church was this, which " to-day is, and
to-morrow is cast into the oven " ? Was my religion
to depend, not merely on a particular interpretation of
1548, but on a particular interpretation of 1918 ?

I do not know at what moment it was that this feeling came over me. I tried to brush it aside at the
time, for I had often argued the case : as far as our
human knowledge went, the Church of England was
sound ; if events proved it otherwise, we should have
to confess that we had been wrong all the time—that
was all. But I could not shake the impression off so
lightly, and the occasion when it overpowered me is
one which I can recall, *quamquam animus meminisse
horret*, to the very day and the very hour. I went up
to London for the morning of St. Augustine's Day, to
see my brother celebrate for the first time at St. Mary's,
Graham Street. We had been brought up together,
known one another at Oxford as brothers seldom do.
It should have been an occasion of the most complete
happiness to see him now, a priest administering for

the first time the most august mystery of our religion,
in the same church, at the same altar, where I had
stood in that position three years before, in his presence.
And then, suddenly, I saw the other side to the
picture.

If this doubt, this shadow of a scruple which had
grown up in my mind, were justifiable—only suppose
it were justifiable, then neither he nor I was a priest,
nor was this the mass, nor was the host the Saving Host;
the accessories of the service—the bright vestments,
the fresh flowers, the mysterious candle-light, were all
settings to a sham jewel; we had been trapped,
deceived, betrayed into thinking it all worth while;
we had ploughed the sand, fought over a phantom
Helen through all these years of conflict. *Nunc alte
vulnus adactum :* there is no such bully as a logical
mind; my intellect, thus peeping down the vistas of
a mere doubt, forced my eyes open to the whole mockery
it involved—and all the time I was supposed to be
worshipping. So far was I, in this agony of realization,
from any holy thoughts, that at the last Gospel I
found only a curse framing itself in my mind; a curse
directed against Henry the Eighth. And so I went up
and kissed the hand of the *neosacerdos.*

I had told my immediate friends—Mr. Child, Mr.
Gurney, Mr. Howell—of the cloud on my horizon
already; in any case, I could not now have kept it back.
I had Mr. Howell's words in my ears all the way back
to Shrewsbury, "Don't break all our hearts." Certainly I must do nothing precipitate, avoid taking
myself too seriously, above all " carry on " as if nothing

had happened. Yet I knew, I think, that I had seen the ghost : the Polar bear (if I may use the less elegant parallel) had vanished, and I was straining my eyes over the heap of clothes. It was at this time that Mr. Moor became my chief confidant, and I his : it was in a letter to him that I enclosed a curious document I still preserve. It contained thirty-one reasons why I should remain an Anglican, and thirty-one reasons why I should become a Roman Catholic, *and all wrong reasons*. My vanity, my ambition, my cowardice, my inertia, all the vices I knew to be in my nature were called in evidence in this diabolic controversy : whatever I did, I maintained, it should not be for these reasons. To illustrate the thoroughness of my introspection, I may instance a single item : "*You had better go over*, because your clothes will attract less attention if you do. *You had better not go over*, because your clothes will attract less attention if you do." Most of the reasons, I need hardly say, were less trivial.

Two duties were obvious. In the first place I wrote to my father, to suggest that I was uneasy in my mind about the Anglican position, though I did not wish to discuss the subject in detail until I should meet him in the summer holidays. In the second place, I told Mr. Alington exactly what I feared : it was not certain what eight weeks of leisure might bring in the way of reconsideration : probably, therefore, it was best that I should not come back in September. That my father's reply was full of sympathy will be easily understood ; Mr. Alington, with the kindest allusions to and avoidance of the theological point at issue, said he was prepared to take all risks, and was urgent that I should come back in September unless by that time I had actually joined the Roman Catholic Communion.

During the latter part of the term and at the be. ginning of the holidays I was still celebrating, preaching, and fulfilling other engagements of a religious kind : I even took a retreat at Oxford, though hearing confessions was, I admit, extraordinarily difficult. I suppose I ought to go into some explanation here. I hope I have made it clear already that my tendency is to mistrust those accesses of religious feeling which Protestant jargon describes as " spiritual experience " —mistrust them, I mean, as *evidence* of religious truth; it is different, of course, with the saints, and with those who are near perfection, but in the case of ordinary people, though I have no doubt God gives them us for our comfort, I would never plead them as evidence of religious truth : I would not say, " Such an overpowering feeling of weakness as I had here is proof positive that the Sacrament which produced it was a valid Sacrament, however much appearances be to the contrary." Emotion plays too large a part in such feelings to make them sure ground for argument. I did not, therefore, at any time believe in Anglican orders on the *a posteriori* evidence of the feelings I had when I made my communion or confession, or celebrated at the altar. My argument was *a priori*, " God wants the Church of England to exist and to fulfil a Catholic mission ; therefore it is natural to suppose that he has not left it without valid Sacra-

ments." Consequently, all the time I believed in the
Church of England I had no "doubts about the
Orders"—such doubts I held to be merely historical
quibbling. But the moment I began to have a glimpse
of the possibility that the Church of England might be
wrong, from that time and to that extent the possibility of the orders being invalid was continually
present to me. It was as if I were suffering from a
kind of astigmatism, my sight so far out of focus that
each eye saw a separate picture : on the one side there
was the possibility that here was a miraculous channel
by which God was bestowing himself on His creatures;
on the other side there was the possibility that—however much nonsacramental grace God was bestowing,
for I had no doubts there—no miracle was taking place,
no convenanted channel of grace being set in motion.
From St. Augustine's Day (of 1915) onwards I never
received or administered a Sacrament without having,
as it were, this double focus in my spiritual vision.

The term came to an end, and one of my first visits
was to Hickleton ; Lord Halifax, at Mr. Howell's
suggestion, had asked me to come and talk over my
difficulties with him. I had looked upon him as my
religious leader for ten years past, and I went gladly
to avail myself of that large-hearted sympathy and
long experience. Mr. Child, who all through this time
and right up to my conversion was continually my
confidant and support, came with me. We came down
to dinner in the fading light of the August evening,
both dressed in cassock and ferraiuolo, priests, it was
impossible not to feel, in a Catholic household. The

first figure I saw in the hall was a familiar one ; it was Father Martindale.

There was no reason why he should not have been there. He was engaged upon Mgr. Benson's Life, and had come to Hickleton for material in connection with the Anglican part of it. (I imagine Hugh Benson had been to Hickleton, in my own errand, twelve years before.) But to meet in this way one of the very few Catholic priests I knew, one for whose powers I had already the utmost respect, seemed too good to be a coincidence. I went and talked to him in his room while he packed (for he was leaving next day), trying to explain my feelings as best I could—that I had lost in these last months the unquestioning consciousness of doing God's will by remaining an Anglican, which had hitherto always been with me, that it had become extremely painful to me to participate in Anglican Sacraments, and so on. I did not come to him for actual direction, but for advice as to whether, in his view, such a state of mind made it right for me, or a duty to me, to shut my eyes and take a plunge. His answer was the last thing I expected : " Of course, you couldn't be received like that."

I need not say that he was perfectly right, but at the moment I caught my breath. I had lived so long in the atmosphere of believing in everything Roman except one—the duty of not being an Anglican—that I had come to imagine the Church of Rome demanded no more as a test of membership than a decent doubt about Anglicanism. It seemed that more was needed ; you could not simply murmur to yourself " *Antiquam exquirite matrem*" and throw yourself into her arms. She demanded positive faith, not a mere dissatisfaction with misbelief. I was to go on, Father Martindale told me, asking for illumination, and using Anglican documents if only as an aid (like the Crusader's piece of grass) to my spiritual communions; at some moment, in answer to my prayers, the point of departure must come, as it comes between sleep and wakefulness when you find yourself ready to get up.

It was (I think) on the Sunday evening of my stay that I went and had my interview with Lord Halifax. The impression I derived from this interview, in which he spoke with the utmost kindness and was clearly anxious not to put any obstacle in the way of my following my own conscience, was that it was a serious matter to abandon lightly the view I had hitherto taken about the mission of the Anglican Church : if you looked at it from that side, the call to labour and fight and suffer in the cause of Corporate Reunion was a thing not easily to be set aside. I promised him, as I had promised Mr. Howell, that I would do nothing hastily, and left Hickleton with the feeling that I was faced with a long time of waiting and of trying to know my own mind.

I went on with Mr. Child to Plymouth, where I was to stay with him. It was two years before that I had preached on *Naboth's Vineyard*, and I read the book again, in the same sunlit room, with the same noise from the open window of the sea sucking against the rocks. With the best will in the world I searched for a strictly logical flaw in it, and failed to find one ; but,

somehow, the whole attitude now seemed unreal. It
was not that there was anything wrong with the book,
there was simply nothing right ; it was like an ingenious mathematical proof deduced from unreal pre-
misses. Mr. Child was urgent with me that I should
not renounce my old position without having some
definite fault to find with it, some new point of view
which would convince himself and others like him that
they had been wrong ; if I must go, let me go in a full
tide of proselytism, not fade away gradually (as he put
it) " like a piece of soap down the sink."

My family were staying at Kington, in Hereford-
shire. It was here that I explained to my father where
I stood ; to him, naturally, it seemed that I was mis-
taking for a call to Rome what was in truth only the
realization that my previous position had been impossible. It was at his suggestion that I read Dr.
Salmon's *Infallibility of the Church*, and wrote to the
Bishop of Exeter, an old friend of his, and a scholar of
distinction, to ask if I might come and take his advice.

Dr. Salmon's book impressed me in two ways. In
the first place, he rests most of his argument not on
history but on dazzling and relentless logic ; the Papal
claim to Infallibility is not simply false, it is inconsistent with itself. Now, this was to meet me with my
own weapons. Faced with a historian, I have to pick
my way with the utmost circumspection, and manœuvre
to get to leeward of him ; to a logician I can stand up,
crossing swords like a man. In a series of annotations
I believed myself to have dealt with him triumphantly,
leaving him to be an atheist if he would, or a spiritualist,

or perhaps a Mormon, but assuredly not a Christian. And he was certainly ingenuous enough to admit that the infallibility of the Church was exactly as difficult to believe in as the Infallibility of the Pope. I had (as I have tried to explain above) always taken for granted that the decisions of the early Councils were directly overruled and therefore in themselves infallible. The Pope's claims were an extra which you might or might not superimpose. Dr. Salmon brought me up against a most uncomfortable fact, on which I had never reflected—namely, *that neither the Bible nor any a priori probability could be adduced as guarantee that an Ecumenical council of Bishops would make infallible decisions.* In other words, so far as authority went, it was just as difficult to be a Tractarian as to be a Roman Catholic.

I tried a little of *Janus* on the Vatican Council, but had to give it up. It was not that I was afraid of being convinced that Rome was wrong: my feeling was that if I went on reading anti-Papal books I should, out of mere reaction, prejudice myself in favour of the Pope. I knew perfectly well that my mind is "contrairy"; it never meets an argument without wanting to rebut it, and usually persuades itself that it has succeeded in doing so: if I had read Littledale and Denny and one or two more, I should have been forced irresistibly Romewards. As a matter of fact, I did not after this read a single book on one side or the other that could be called purely controversial, right up to the time of my submission. Instead, I tried the more spacious method of history. Acting on the admirable advice of Mr. Williams, I read Eusebius in the Greek and the first volume of Duchesne; this was to give me a candid idea of whether the early Church was Papalist or not. Now, I do not pretend that on coming on it from the outside the evidence as between a Gallican and a Papalist interpretation of the first three centuries is definitely cogent, to myself at any rate: if there were no other factors to be taken into consideration, I would simply say that the evidence was capable of either interpretation. (So I have heard Dr. Darwell Stone say, if I do not misrepresent him, from the Anglican side.) But I think the actual effect of Eusebius on me was to enhance my idea of the importance of the early Papacy. Both for the Newcastle at school and for my ordination examinations I had been content to read strictly Anglican handbooks, and these, I suppose, burked the Roman question instead of arguing about it. Since then I had come to believe that I believed in the Papacy, but whether on grounds of continuous tradition or of development I never stopped to inquire. Now, as I revised the whole question, it did strike me that the Papal claims, even if they were not always admitted, were at least very early made; the early Fathers might deny or assert them, but at least they did not, like the handbooks, hide them away. So imperfect an impression do the handbooks leave that I actually had not realized that St. Athanasius appealed to Rome. Yet I did not, at this time or later, devote any very minute study to the isolated texts which have been so eagerly discussed, except that I sent to Father Sharpe, of More Hall (who was studying this period) my views about one reference in St. Ignatius, and one in St. Irenaeus.

But meanwhile it became clear to me, since I had read Salmon, that my whole position needed a thorough overhauling : was I sure that the Presbyterians were not right ? Or even the Society of Friends ? I began, therefore, to put my views on paper, imitating, as far as possible, the manner of Aristotle. I mean, I tried to take as my data general principles about the idea of a Church such as everybody would be disposed to recognize, and then correlate them and bring out their implications. This method, from a literary point of view so much less interesting than the Platonic, is far better suited for the purposes of one who is not sure of his own mind, and has to give random hours and half-hours, instead of continuous days of investigation, to his subject.

All this time (August, 1915), while this turmoil of questionings was raging in my head, blow after blow was dealt me from without by tragic news of my best friends. Most of these had joined Kitchener's First Army, the army of Hooge and of the Suvla landing. I could hardly read a paper or open a post without a fresh stab that threatened to shake my whole faith to its roots. One satisfaction I had ; for even then I felt it as a satisfaction. A little time before, I suppose about the end of the summer term, Mr. E. R. Hicks, whom I had long known as a friend and recently became connected with by family inter-marriage, had written from Gallipoli to tell me that he was contemplating submission to Rome ; he had had troubles before, and I think that the piety of the Irish troops to which he found himself attached produced a strong impression. My advice to him was still what it had been to B earlier on, that I was in no position to advise. I think it was about the end of the summer holidays that he wrote to me from Egypt announcing his reception into the Church.

From Kington I went, as I had arranged, to Exeter, where the Bishop entertained me with the utmost kindness and devoted most of a long September day to the consideration of my difficulties. On the point which now troubled me most—namely, the difficulty of finding a divine sanction for the decrees of the Councils, on which I had rested so much—he surprised me by taking what I had always considered a rather Modernist line ; it was not, he argued, the *ipse dixit* of Nicea or Chalcedon, but the subsequent acceptance by the whole Church (laity and all) of those decisions which determined their authority. I tried for a time to content myself with this view, but it seemed to me (I am not now speaking of the actual interview) that " acceptance by the Church " was a very dangerous weapon in Anglican hands ; if we said that the whole Church accepted the doctrine of the Single Person in the Incarnation, meaning thereby that the Nestorians went into schism, could not something very much like it be said of the Council of Trent ? And I must say that if acceptance by the Church is the real test, it seems to me the prerogatives of the Papacy are not merely ratified but enthusiastically proclaimed by the popular voice, whereas the doctrine of the Incarnation is a theological definition to which the mass of the faithful gives only an unintellectual assent. On the *consensus fidelium* argument two difficulties seemed to me unsurmountable : (1) Are the Nestorians *fideles* ? And if not, why not ? (2) Are the Presbyterians *fideles* ? And if not, why not ?

This came later : I must return to the interview. The Bishop did me the honour of suggesting that God had given me an intellectual apparatus superior to those of many around me ; therefore it was my duty to take whatever step I took not rashly or suddenly, but with thought and circumspection. That did not mean that I was to "get up" the Roman controversy ; it would be far better that I should read Church History in a leisurely way from some Gallican (and therefore neutral) authority ; he named some books that might be suitable. " Read round the subject " was the gist of his advice, and though I did not stick to its letter I think I can say I acted in the spirit of it.

My friend, Charles Lister, was killed that autumn. In corresponding with his sister, Lady Lovat (whom I had not met since her conversion and marriage), I told her of my difficulties ; she was the first Catholic (after Father Martindale) to whom I had done so. I also hinted at them in writing to the Abbot of Caldey, and not long afterwards to Mr. Urquhart, of Balliol, otherwise I had no Catholic confidants except a few who had recently been Anglicans like myself. Mr. Wilfrid Moor was received that autumn. Captain Scott-Moncrieff, who (like Mr. Hicks) asked for my final advice, had already been received in France.

Mr. Hicks and B I have mentioned. *O fortunati, quorum jam moenia surgunt!* I was deep enough in my doubts to be envious of them.

Before I went back to Shrewsbury I applied for advice in one other quarter. Mr. Mackay, of Margaret Street, had done me many kindnesses, and I knew that the loss of Mr. Moor would make him sympathetic. His advice was psychological and practical : the war, he said, had put all our nerves on the stretch, and we did not realize at what a high pitch of tension we were living. Might not my own case be simply one of " war-nerves " ? And, for fear of that, would it not be best to wait till the end of the war ? I made the obvious answer, and he said, " Surely two years from now." If I took nobody else's advice, I was faithful to his. My brother also inclined to the " war-nerves " theory, and urged that I ought to take up parish work to occupy my mind. Mr. Kilburn, of St. Saviour's, Hoxton, was good enough to suggest my going there and trying the effect of seeing my old religion at work. The same advice, it will be remembered, was given to Hugh Benson. " He might equally well have told me to go and teach Buddhism." I did not feel so strongly as that, but I was quite certain that I could not hear confessions, and ought not to preach. My last preaching engagement I fulfilled that September at Froyle, near Alton : the Vicar of St. Martin's, Cardiff, had already been kind enough to release me from my promise to conduct the Three Hours on Good Friday. I would seek, at Shrewsbury, for spiritual rest and for work which could not trouble my conscience.

P

XIII

GOLDEN CHAINS

Ardet abire fuga, dulcesque relinquere terras
Attonitus tanto monitu.

I DESPAIR of being able to convey any impression of the next fourteen months, up to the Christmas of 1916. If I try to give any full picture of my life, it will necessarily be irrelevant to my main topic : if I simply follow up the history of my inward developments I shall give a quite false because arbitrarily selected picture. The truth is that I lived in two distinct compartments at Shrewsbury : in my relations with those round me, I must have appeared simply as a clergyman of eccentric views, taking a long holiday from most of the official practices of religion, and thinking of nothing except how to make himself agreeable ; nor was this hypocritical, for while I was with other people this was exactly what I was. But give me half an hour by myself, with no work pressing, and I would plunge at once into self-questioning, brooding, and something not unlike despair. The headmaster, as I have said, was in my confidence, and I imagine that Mrs. Alington suspected something of what I felt ; only one of the masters, to my knowledge, realized the situation : the others may or may not have guessed something, but I never

said a word. Not even in the holidays did I unbosom
myself to anybody except a few trusted friends. It
was not that I wanted the thing kept dark, it was
simply that my conscience had become like a sore
tooth, too irritable to be laid bare or to be probed
without a further access of pain ; it shrank into itself
and kept its own secret.

It was, chiefly, from this instinct of reticence, but
partly also because I felt it as an impertinence to in-
flict my own troubles upon others, that I did not even
declare myself to my superiors outside Shrewsbury—
to the President of Trinity, I mean, and the Bishop
of Oxford. My visits to Oxford became fewer, and I
had not even the occasion to consult my regular confessor there, Father Maxwell. I knew exactly what
he felt about Rome, and that his clearly-cut views
were views I could not share. He died in the spring of
1916, and I felt a fresh break with the past.

Externally, my life at Shrewsbury was very fully
occupied. My form was a middle form which served
impartially as a brief stepping-stone for the ambitious
and as a grateful backwater for the disillusioned—
one of the difficulties of examinations was to deal with
the people who deliberately " sugared " for fear of
promotion. Hence their ages ranged from fourteen to
nineteen, and their intellects over an even wider field.
Mr. Southwell, a born teacher because a born enthu-
siast, had cast a spell over them by the infection of his
love for poetry and for the classics. I, his successor,
had just lost all the motive power which had hitherto
directed my life : I was stale and blasé as well as

tutorially incompetent. The only thing to do was to
throw myself into a desperate endeavour to keep my
form amused and happy : this must be my intellectual
circle, my public, my congregation. I discarded as
far as possible the use of exercise books, and produced
all my own exercises, as well as my own " copies " on
the hektograph ; to be able to provide a continual
succession of surprises and of amusements was the
sole purpose of my existence. On a day of full work
I would be working from first lesson in the morning
till midnight, or after midnight, with no interval
except for meals and for reading my office, and every
moment of it, except when my form showed signs of
boredom in school, was unadulterated pleasure.
Punishment, from inertia, not from disapproval, I
rarely imposed, and still more rarely exacted ; the
continual feeling of humiliation which I had in myself
discouraged the desire to criticize or condemn others.
On their side, they certainly did not overwork, and I
do not think they learned much, but if they found me
a joke they at least thought me a good-natured one,
and a feeling of something warmer than mere mutual
toleration grew up between us. Sitting in the deep
window-sill, while the evening mists began to rise
from the adorable curve of the Severn that flows under
the schools, I watched them wrestling with some intolerably eccentric piece of composition in an inde-
scribable atmosphere of electic light, crumpled paper,
and chalk-dust, twenty independent lives not bur-
dened with my knowledge, not troubled with my
speculations, enough of human contact to preserve me

from mere self-centredness or from the abandonment of despair.

It is a commonplace frequently agreed upon by symposia of elderly stockbrokers in drearily immaculate clubs that schoolmasters are a type, a machine-made product, destitute of any save false enthusiasms, out of touch with the world around them, slaves of the groove and wholly given over to pedantry. The explanation is simple ; *maxima debetur pueris reverentia*, and an even greater to parents ; to a boy, the schoolmaster is what the boy thinks he ought to be, to the parent what the parent thinks he ought to be ; meanwhile, he has a soul, and only those who have been schoolmasters and been on intimate terms with their colleagues can really know the facts. Of the junior masters at Shrewsbury (I speak for these only, because I know them the best) I can honestly say that I never came in contact in all my life with a group of minds so original. Mr. Southwell and Mr. White, who both left just before I came and have both since been killed at the front, left behind them a language and a tradition full of the strangest eccentricities and of the most penetrating humour. I must spare the blushes of the living by leaving the record of their praises a blank, and let the stockbroker continue in his ignorance ; I only wish he could have been present at some of our discussions on war-aims.

I lived in a small colony with three other masters. The house, being centrally placed, was a good deal frequented by the other bachelors of the staff. In various moods, the stranger (coming in to ask for the key

of the bicycle-shed) might have taken the house for a
pandemonium, or he might have taken it for an
opium-den : I do not think he could ever have accused
us of pedagogic ultra-correctness. Planning of corps
field-days in prospect and enjoyment of them in retrospect, chaotic strugglings with belated exercises or
with a refractory hektograph, barbarous auditions
from the gramophone, long arguments on anything and
on nothing conducted in the most preposterous atti-
tudes and with the strongest variations of an esoteric
argot, three-hour and four-hour games of *L'Attaque*,
at which one or two of us were furious adepts, shoutings
and stampings and causeless ringing of bells, alternating
with extraordinary periods of sleepiness and discontent with the world in general—our life "seemed full as
it could hold," and Heaven knows I enjoyed myself.
But as I lay wakeful at night, or wandered up and
down the garden trying to make my meditation, or
listened, envious but aloof, to the shouts of encouragement and of triumph from distant football fields,
there was always the *amari aliquid* in my heart, the
restless demon at my side. The tenure on which I
held my earthly happiness was one of spiritual indecision—at what point would this indecision become
culpable ?

Father Martindale once suggested, in writing to me,
that if you did not find yourself arriving at "getting-
up point" in the morning by natural process, it sometimes became necessary to put force upon yourself and
bring yourself up to the scratch ; I think he was afraid
that I might be waiting about listlessly for a divine

illumination. I told him that at least I was not conscious of going back ; my ears were still strained to catch
any call : I think this was quite true, even when I was
busiest. But what troubled me at Shrewsbury was not
so much the material comfort of my surroundings, or
the immense happiness (from a human point of view)
I was deriving from my work, as the sense that by per-
severing in this attitude of uncertainty I was shirking
the strain of " mental fight " to which I had been
accustomed. It was so easy to be charitable to people
of other beliefs, when you were not sure that they were
false. It was so easy to be tolerant of other people's
misdemeanours, when you were not quite sure that a
fixed standard existed for judging right and wrong.
When I was at Balliol, we used to adapt the phrase
" I hold no brief for So-and-so " in a positive way :
thus we said that Charles Lister held a brief for
Socialism, Julian Grenfell a brief for sport, and so on.
At that time (having several " briefs " of my own) I
used to argue that to hold no briefs was to be less than
a man. Ever since then I had been fighting for a
cause, ready to argue a point, eager to make converts.
Now I found myself briefless : I did not know what
cause I wanted to win ; I could argue on most subjects
dispassionately ; I did not know what to convert
people to. Many people would say that this attitude
was infinitely preferable to my previous attitude. I
admit that I think the period of " lying fallow " from
controversy may have been good for my temper : if
so, I thank God for it : but I did not and do not
believe that it is good for a man to remain for long in

this boneless and flabby condition of mind. I felt that my friends were wondering how an extreme High Churchman, the author of several very polemical works, could be so broad-minded : I could not explain, but cursed myself for my broad-mindedness.

I have already explained that I refused all this time to occupy a pulpit. You might, I argued, have enough personal conviction, or lack of conviction, to struggle on in the darkness, availing yourself of Sacraments which meant little to you ; but you could not preach or instruct unless you had the certainty of God-given authority behind you. For, as Plato says, there can be no greater sin than misleading a fellow-creature into false belief : I was conscious of the cross-grained texture of my own intellect, and would run no risks of leading the blind. One office, however, I did consent to undertake. Mr. Alington had introduced the custom of ten-minute " talks " after Evensong on Sundays : they were not delivered from the pulpit, they were not even necessarily religious as distinct from ethical ; once, I think, he read them the end of Plato's apology in a translation. Several of his own " talks " have been published by him under the name of *Shrewsbury Fables*. I did not scruple to address the school under such conditions ; and the levity of phrase and of illustration which had sometimes made churchwardens look askance at me was treasured delightedly by my new audience. Having no positive principles of my own to enounce, the burden of my message was generally that, whatever principles you had, they must be positive ones : I also tried to attract

the sympathy of my audience towards the supernatural as opposed to the (more popular) natural
virtues : I remember, for example, drawing a damaging comparison between San Celestino and Mr. Pem-
berton Billing. But I would not preach in the
mornings, nor did I accept engagements elsewhere,
except once when a country vicar, the father of two
Salopians, was called away unavoidably for a Sunday
and could find no substitute.

From the religious life of the school I felt curiously
aloof. I went usually, though not regularly, to the
service on week-day mornings, and often to that on
Sunday evenings : my attendance at the early celebration on Sundays was regular, for to this (as long as I
was an Anglican) I felt myself bound. Now, I had
quite lost all relish for vestments and ceremonial and
the trammels of worship ; so long as Peter's shrine
was empty, the Church was all one for me. The chapel
services, though not much different in ecclesiastical
tone from those of most public schools, were sensible,
short (as compared with many I have known), and
varied beyond the strict letter of the Prayer Book ;
the chapel (Mr. Alington argued) was a peculiar. Nothing could have been better calculated to wean my mind
back to ordinary Anglicanism ; there was no fussiness,
no parochialism, no sense of artificial moderation. The
hymns were plentiful, and such as I liked ; the ambitions set before the boys were high and unselfish ;
Mr. Alington's preaching was, as I had known it in
Eton days, at once brilliant and easy of comprehen-
sion. Yet the feeling which the services chiefly inspired

in me was one of profound melancholy ; I was a mere
spectator, cut off from the religion around me by some
mysterious self-imprisonment of the conscience. I
could not pray in chapel, I could only watch people
pray and rejoice that they were doing it.

I had not, of course, given up my own prayers. I
never abandoned the recitation of the Divine Office ;
often I had to read it while I was invigilating over the
work of my pupils, but I was not fearful of scandaliz-
ing them, for at the worst they would probably be no
wiser than the Trinity undergraduate, who said that
when he came into my room he always found me
learning the Prayer Book by heart. But beyond this,
whenever my work allowed, I did my best to make a
half-hour meditation, grievously distracted as a rule by
the troubles that exercised me, but devoted to the
intention of obtaining light. It was the Psalms of
David I chiefly used, and found extraordinary comfort in certain phrases of them : " *Expecta Dominum,
viriliter age, et confortetur cor tuum, et sustine Dominum,*" " *Deus meus es tu, quoniam bonorum meorum non
eges,*" " *Spera in Domino et fac bonitatem, et inhabita
terram, et pasceris in divitiis eius,*" and so on. But,
with all the grace then given me, I did not find it easy
to win satisfaction in prayer.

I had little time for reading during the term, and
what reading I did during odd half-hours was mostly
of a quite light type, not calculated to affect my
religious views. (Mr. Southwell had a principle that
everybody ought to read Mr. Belloc's *Path to Rome*
every autumn ; I reread it twice at Shrewsbury, set

it as a holiday task to my form, and while at home enriched it with an index under more than three hundred heads ; but it is not exactly propaganda.) But I had the Christmas and Easter holidays ; and, further, I had to have an operation during the Lent term, and was in bed a full three weeks : all this time I utilized pretty fully. In pursuance, therefore, of the Eusebius-Duchesne principle, and of Bishop Robertson's advice, I " read round " the subject of the Papacy and the Reformation ; also I made a definite effort to get a sympathetic view of standpoints other than my own. Among the books I so read were Creighton's *History of the Papacy* (in six volumes), Gairdner's *Lollardy and the Reformation* (in four very large volumes), three or four volumes of Milman's *History of Latin Christianity*, Ward's *Life of Newman*, Pater on the Renaissance, the Master of Balliol on Church and State in the Middle Ages, Sir James Stephen on the Portroyalists, a volume of Acton's Lectures, Church's *History of the Oxford Movement*, Balleine's *History of the Evangelical Party*, Newman (as an Anglican) on the Arians, and an introduction (I think by Bishop Lightfoot) to St. Cyprian. It will be seen that, at the best, it is a Gallican view of the Church which these selections represent, and I do not think I can be accused of " cramming myself up with Jesuit stuff." (I did, however, read Father Martindale's Life of Hugh Benson in the summer.)

From all this reading I derived a wealth of impressions, but I think the only sudden access of illumination I got was from a phrase in Milman's (soundly

Protestant) *History of Latin Christianity.* I cannot
remember it well enough to quote it, but the gist of it
is this ; he comments upon the extraordinary precision
with which, time after time, the Bishops of Rome
managed to foresee which side the Church would
eventually take in a controversy, and " plumped "
for it beforehand. The Church fixes the date of Easter,
the Church decides that heretics need not be rebap-
tized, the Church decides that the Incarnate combined
two Natures in one Person ; but each time Rome (like
Lancashire) thinks to-day what the world will think
to-morrow. This uncanny capacity for taking the
pulse of the Church is ascribed by Milman partly to
the extreme cunning of the early Pontiffs, partly to
their geographically central position, and so on. And
then it occurred to me that there was another explanation. I could have laughed aloud.

Strange as it may seem, I had always assumed at
the back of my mind that when my handbooks talked
about " Arian " and " Catholic " bishops they knew
what they were talking about ; it never occurred to
me that the Arians also regarded themselves as Catholics and wanted to know why they should be thought
otherwise. " Ah ! but," says my Church historian,
" the Church came to think otherwise, and thus they
found themselves de-Catholicized in the long run."
But what Church ? Why did those who anathematized Nestorius come to be regarded as " Catholics "
rather than those who still accept his doctrines ? I
had used this argument against the attitude of the
Greek Orthodox Church when it broke away from

unity, but it had never occurred to me before that *what we mean when we talk of the Catholic party is the party in which the Bishop of Rome was, and nothing else:* that the handbooks had simply taken over the word without thinking or arguing about it, as if it explained itself ; but it didn't.

I am desperately afraid here of not stating my meaning clearly : what it comes to is this. I had been in the habit of supposing that the Nestorians were wrong because East and West agreed that they were wrong ; I now felt that " the East " had no right to condemn the Nestorians, it was merely a matter of " hard swearing "—except in so far as the Easterns, when they did so, had the Pope in their own boat. If you ask " Who are the Orthodox ? " you will be told " The people who hold the Orthodox Faith." If you ask them how they know it is the Orthodox Faith they say " Because it is held by the Orthodox Church." And the Nestorians will say exactly the same of themselves—and who is to choose between them ? Each say that they have the *consensus fidelium* behind them, and if you ask who the *fideles* were you are referred back to the very formula which the *consensus fidelium* was to prove. But if you ask a Catholic " What is the Catholic Faith ? " and are told it is that held by the Catholic Church ; if you persevere, and ask what is the Catholic Church, you are no longer met with the irritatingly circular definition " the Church which holds the Catholic Faith " ; you are told it is the Church which is in communion with the Bishop of Rome.

When I had got so far, my solution of the difficulties

was this. If you did not believe in authority at all, but only believed in the " experience of Christendom," the Papacy seemed to be *the* thing which mediæval Christendom was certain about, and the loss of which Christendom (if you use the term in a wide sense) had been largely engaged in mourning for ever since. If you took your authority from the Councils, you were faced with the fact that the Councils were only decided by majorities, and the obvious majority of Christendom came to believe (if it did not believe already) in the Pope. If you took your stand on the *consensus fidelium*, you must either despair of defining the *fideles*, or else define them as the people who kept touch with the centre of Unity, that is, with the Pope. If you took a Gallican view of the Church, and wanted the Papacy to be a constitutional monarchy, your church became a philosopher's dream instead of a living reality : in ordinary real life you must have the Pope as he is, or no Pope at all. All these efforts which men have made at various times to invent a substitute for the full Petrine claims were simply zigzag paths which came to the same thing in the end ; they all led to Rome. Modernism, and Tractarianism, and Consensus-fideliumism, and Gallicanism all demanded a Pope ; and there was no Pope to be had unless you went one better than any of them. It reminded me of a random walk I once took in London, when, turn into side alleys as I would, I still found the great campanile of Westminster looming up in front of me, and I felt in myself that it was saying " I'll have you yet."

And my difficulty was this—I had had no new

light, no sudden revelation. All these considerations I have been recounting had been, for several
years, familiar to me as the back of my hand. And all
this time I had not drawn a Roman Catholic conclusion from them : how was it that I had altered ? If I
was wrong then, how could I be certain I was not
wrong now ? If I was right now, how could I be certain I was not right then ? Might not my whole
present outlook be (as Newman says) " an abuse of
the intellect," a great bubble which, if I only waited,
would break suddenly and leave me to my old realities
again ? If I had made an intellectual step forward,
I could have welcomed the new progress and con-
formed myself to the new developments ; but I had
taken no new intellectual step : I saw the same set of
facts, and my intellect made an entirely different
report of them. For years my ten spies had told me
that the promised land was impossible of entrance ;
how could I trust Joshua and Caleb when they had
had the same evidence at their disposal, and came
back with the assurance that the promised land was
mine ?

In this intolerable distrust of my own intellectual
process I lay, miserable and inert. At times it seemed
to me that the Church of England was a prison which
would not let me go.

Castra inimica vides, nulla hinc exire potestas.

At other times, and more frequently, it seemed to me
that the Church of Rome had spread a great net round
me, of meshes too fine to be seen, yet too stout to be

broken through : I was beating my head against them in vain. Again and again I have wondered at myself for not slipping back, by sheer spiritual exhaustion, into my old ways of thought and my old easy contentment. I suppose it must have been the Poor Clares, whom Father Martindale had asked to pray for me, and those others who weré praying for me unasked, that pulled me back every time and kept me face to face with my despairs.

In the event, I came to the conclusion that I must leave Shrewsbury. On the one side, if I was destined to become a Roman Catholic, to stay at Shrewsbury was to tie myself down with another bond very difficult to break : already the step would mean the wrench of leaving Oxford and Anglicanism, it was coming to be a wrench to leave Shrewsbury as well. I could not afford to be tied down with the golden chains of that delightful leisure and yet more delightful industry. On the other side, if I was meant to be a Romanizing Anglican once more, it might be that my quiet life there, during which I never saw a copy of the *Church Times* or had news of the latest controversy, never celebrated, and seldom made my Confession or Communion, were inducing in me a general slackness of the spirit ; I was perhaps running to seed. In the course of that summer Mr. Howell, my considerate friend and benefactor, my confessor now so far as I had one, died unexpectedly as the result of an operation. Graham Street would be short of curates, and I could give my help. About the same time, one of my elder brothers suggested my taking up work in a department of the

War Office under which he was himself employed :
here, it seemed, was a chance of spending my summer
holiday in useful activity. I would deny myself a
holiday, go up to London, work at the War Office,
help at Graham Street, and perhaps afterwards
arrange for the engagement to be permanent.

This programme I carried out, living most of August
and September with Mr. Child, who was then a curate
at Holy Trinity, Sloane Street. The authorities of the
department were anxious that I should not return to
Shrewsbury at all, but I felt myself under an engagement to Mr. Alington, and he was urgent that I should
go back for that term. At the end of that term
(i.e. at Christmas) he himself was leaving, having been
appointed to the Headmastership of Eton. In the
course of the Somme battle Mr. Southwell, whose
place I was taking, was killed in action. My contract
at Shrewsbury might thus have been held to be at an
end, but this consideration would not, *ceteris paribus*,
have weighed with me for a moment ; Shrewsbury
had entered into me ; I loved every stone of it ; its
ways, its atmosphere, its society had come to be part
of the machinery of my life. But the very calm of my
life there might, it seemed to me, be a treacherous
calm, for after all I was still in mid-ocean:

Urbem orant, taedet pelagi perferre laborem;

whether it were the Carthage that had begun to feel
unreal to me, or the Rome that seemed as far as ever
from my reach, a city I must have, streets busy with
labour, and walls that challenged attack.

Q

I did not, even then, explain to my friends my reasons for leaving ; the very intention I only let out by accident, and they must have thought me singularly ungracious. Only to Canon Sawyer, the new Headmaster, who both then and afterwards showed me the utmost understanding and sympathy, did I explain the difficulty of staying on. I knew that I must put a period to my indecision, and if my determination should fall Romewards, I would not have the reputation of Shrewsbury suffer an instant by my defection. The term wore on, and on the last Sunday but one I prepared for my last address in Sunday evening chapel. I took for my subject "The Parting of Friends" : I do not know if any of my audience realized what I had in my mind. The boys certainly did not ; they felt that I was not so frivolous as usual, and wore a suppressed air of demanding their money back. One omen came to me as I sat composing my address. I was describing the loneliness of a soul forced by conscientious motives to detach itself from loved surroundings and familiar friendships, and launch out into the deep. A Virgilian quotation naturally suggested itself :

Nec jam amplius ullae
Apparent terrae, maria undique, et undique caelum;

and as I wrote it down, another reading of the line flashed across my mind : "MARIA undique, et undique CAELUM." Perhaps I was not so lonely after all.

It is open to anybody to say that during these four last terms of my stay at Shrewsbury I was drugging my conscience, giving myself up to self-pleasing, skulking in idleness. I have no wish to justify myself, but if it is true, I confess that my affection for the place, and the life of the place, and the friends I made there blinds me to my delinquency. If I unlearnt there some of my intolerance for the vagueness of other people's minds, some of my impatience with the slowness of other people's decisions, if I learnt to expect little and to praise the little good where I found it, that is after all part of a life's education, and perhaps God saw I needed it. At least the memory of the tree-fringed river, and the pencilled snows on Caradoc, autumn mists and bright firesides, boys melancholy as only boys can be, and cheerful as only boys have a right to be, besides a thousand kindnesses which ingratitude forgets or friendship would not let me betray, make my Shrewsbury life as far outside my nature to regret as it was beyond my capacities to forgo.

XIV

EBURY STREET

Heu vatum ignarae mentes ! Quid vota furentem,
Quid delubra juvant ? Est molles flamma medullas
Interea, et tacitum vivit sub pectore vulnus.

AT the beginning of January, then, I came back to
London. My work at the War Office occupied me
for the whole of the day except on Saturdays and Sundays, and I cannot accuse myself of idleness. I was
living, meanwhile, first in lodgings near Sloane Square,
and then with Mr. Child and Mr. Baker in Ebury
Street. Sometimes, but rarely, I went away for week-
ends, but generally speaking I was tied down to
London for these nine months.

I gave what help I could at St. Mary's, Graham
Street. I would not preach, much less hear Confessions,
but I had no objection to celebrating, so long as my
position was clearly understood, and I suppose I was
at the altar not less than three times a week. It made
me acutely miserable, for all the time (and especially
at the Consecration) the possibility that I was not a
priest and consequently not sacrificing danced continuously before my eyes. But (it seemed to me) I
had had enough at Shrewsbury of spiritual rest-cure ;
to be away from ecclesiastical interests and apart from
sacerdotal functions had not succeeded in shaking me
down into my old ways of thought : the only thing
that remained was to try and persuade myself, by the

exercise of the powers I claimed, of my right to claim them. Perhaps, in the doing of it, my spiritual outlook would be adjusted once more. Never for a moment, as a matter of fact, did any such feeling come to me.

I was now back in my old surroundings as exactly as could be conceived. Mr. Howell had been succeeded by my friend Mr. Whitby (till then a curate at Haggerston), who not only shared my old views but belonged to the particular circle in which I had been accustomed to move. My brother remained as his curate, and Mr. Child had joined them. Mr. Howell's doctrines and tastes had always been in sympathy with ours; and whatever alterations were made in the services, chiefly designed to make them shorter, were popular, and more frequent, all seemed to me (or would have seemed to me three years before, I cannot tell which) so much to the good. The Church itself was my favourite church in London, and was for me the centre of many kindly associations. Other like-minded priests were our guests from time to time. In the summer, Mr. Williams was much in the neighbourhood. As Shrewsbury was remote from, so Ebury Street was closely allied to, the traditions of my past. Not only that, but the movement I had once championed so eagerly was on the march; the Bishops, instead of squabbling with us over the use of incense, were actually divided as to whether the Blessed Sacrament might or might not be reserved in circumstances tending to its adoration: and that Corpus Christi Day I saw for the first time (on a visit to another parish) the Host carried in procession through London streets. And I found myself condemned to look on helpless, like some public-school football hero under doctor's orders, watching *the* match of the season from a bath-chair. I might compose a hymn, now and then, or make some liturgical suggestion, but neither my conscience nor my feelings would let me take part in any controversy or agitation.[1] I was a spectator, and I found myself even becoming a critic.

Meanwhile, the Church of Rome held out to me no sensible attraction whatever. I do not merely mean that her ritual and ceremonial, with all their dignity and beauty, could not act as a bait : this must have been true at any time for anybody of my school. In Tractarian days the historic worship of the Church may have been an allurement ; but we had been accustomed to so accurate a reproduction of it all that it had lost the charm of novelty, and lacked besides the excitement of being illicit. Picture the schoolboy, who after terms of surreptitious smoking, when the necessity of precaution and the consciousness of being a " sportsman " were elements in his pleasure as real as the fragrance of the tobacco itself, presented by an aunt, on going up to a university, with a new pipe and tobacco-pouch. Something of the same blasé appreciation makes itself felt in the mind of the modern Anglican extremist when he is invited to admire Catholic services ; he has not merely done all this before, he has done it defiantly, deliberately, with the joy of contest to encourage him.

[1] I did sign one petition, but it was one which commanded some thoroughly respectable signatures.

It was not, I say, merely that : the whole system gave me no pleasure to contemplate. I had always thought of " poping " (to use the familiar term) as something which, if you were bound to do it, you did with alacrity and perhaps even relief : the step-off would be as easy as that from a moving staircase on to a platform : you had all the apparatus in you for believing Catholic doctrines, and you had only to put it in motion : you had always been admiring Roman Catholicism from a distance, now you had merely to stand forward and claim it as your own. It may have been from " lying fallow " at Shrewsbury so long ; but in the actual event, when I came to contemplate submission to the Church as a concrete step, I found not a trace of this alacrity in myself. I turned towards my Mother, and she had grown strange to me. All the doctrines I had thought I believed (for myself I am content to say, had believed) all these years—the miracle of the Mass, the Immaculate Conception, the Power of the Keys, and so on—I now seemed to be approaching *de novo*, as if from a standpoint of agnosticism. Use had robbed them of their mysterious charm, but seemed no longer to make the belief in them easy or natural to me. No isolated doctrines were real or vivid ; I was all one great aching bruise, cared about nothing except one point—was I in communion with the Church Christ ordained ? If not, could I conscientiously resign myself to the action which, if anything would, would make me so ?

Gradually, the question narrowed itself down ; I was conscious that I *could* not force myself back into my old position, and it only remained to ask, Could I conscientiously join the only institution which looked like the Church of Christ, or must I remain outside, retaining perhaps in myself some half-light of faith, but unable to teach, to proselytize, or to assert? Catholics who find such an alternative even abstractly unthinkable should take note of Mr. Shane Leslie's article on Florence Nightingale in the *Dublin Review* of October, 1917. They will see there that it is possible for a soul to become dissatisfied with Anglicanism through long turning of the eyes Romewards, yet find herself unable to enter into that rest for which (St. Augustine tells us) her struggles are evidence that she was created.

It was in this frame of mind that I talked to Father Martindale again, when I went to Oxford at the beginning of Lent, and he now told me that I had nothing to gain by waiting; I ought to go away for a day or two and be received at Easter. My answer was that I could not hope to resolve my difficulties so suddenly; I must go properly into retreat. This, from the circumstances of my office work, would not be possible until I took my fortnight's holiday in the summer. This holiday I had already ear-marked for the purpose: I would go away and face my terrors, and return as a Catholic or as a baffled aspirant to Catholicism. I think, from my subsequent experiences, that I could safely have trusted Father Martindale's advice.

I had no longer the feeling I had at Shrewsbury; rather the opposite. There, I had been pulled each way simultaneously; happiness counselled delay, adventurousness called for action ; the only difficulty was the decision

Miserum inter amorem
Praesentis terrae, fatisque vocantia regna.

Now, I felt no pull either way, but complete inertia. I was incapable of making any overtures to Anglicanism, not for lack of will, nor from weariness with my old pursuits ; I was conscious simply of a negative scruple that would not let me go back ;

Di me terrent, et Juppiter hostis.

Yet there was no corresponding impulse forward ; I had become habituated to indecision, and found in myself no positive craving for light ; the glamour of the Seven Hills had died away. This was what troubled me : could it be right to come to the feast, even out of the highways and hedges, with no feeling in my heart except ennui ? Yet I did not dare to believe that my prayers, hampered by so many distractions, could merit the imparting of any sudden illumination : I travelled daily to Charing Cross with no hope that I should catch a glimpse of the traffic of Jacob's Ladder. Nor, on the other side, did I find that I was naturally approaching a crisis ; that after so long kicking against the goad I should reach the point of saying,

Non vires alias, conversaque numina sentis ?
Cede Deo.

There seemed no reason why my present state of mind should not continue indefinitely.

" Should," I mean, in the sense of probability : in

the sense of duty, I was more doubtful. It needs a very good conscience indeed to be able to say that you have corresponded with every access of grace, left no opportunity ungrasped, that you are not to blame for your own doubts. I suggested in writing to a friend that perhaps I would be allowed into heaven on the plea of invincible indecision, but I was not in truth very hopeful. The air-raid season, at times, affected me with tremors not merely physical; I was not certain that I wanted to meet the Particular Judgment. More, I began to be afraid of a retrograde motion. My wise friend Father Figgis, of Mirfield, when I saw him at Shrewsbury during the summer of 1916, had clearly been of opinion that I had better leave the Church of England than remain in it long in my then state of mind. " You haven't," he told me, " a temperament that you can afford to play with." It seemed to me that the loss of faith, and even the loss of moral standards, would neither be an unnatural result of my hesitation, nor, if it were culpable, an inappropriate punishment for it. I met Father Figgis again in London, and he still held to his view.

I felt, therefore, that I could not be accused of forcing God's hand or voluntarily turning my back on my old home if I tied myself down to a fixed date : a date, not for being received, but for putting myself in a Roman Catholic atmosphere and considering my difficulties with all the aid such an atmosphere would afford me. Meanwhile, there were ties that still had to be severed. My personal ties, indeed, were diminished in number. Of the undergraduates for whose religious development I regarded myself as responsible, B and Mr. Hicks had become Catholics; of C's position I have already spoken. One of the others had been killed at Loos, another at the Somme; another, captured at Kut, was a prisoner in the hands of the Turks. But I was still a Fellow of Trinity, and had not given my colleagues there any intimation of a change in my sentiments. In June I received notice that my Fellowship would come up for reconfirmation at Michaelmas, as I should have held it for seven years; tutorial fellowships are reconfirmed without difficulty except in unusual circumstances, and I suppose it is likely that mine would have been. I wrote to the President, told him the whole history of the last two years, and asked him to inform the College that I did not aspire to re-election. His answer was most generous; he did not personally think that I should find in Rome the satisfaction of my doubts, and he was anxious that I should not be precipitate, but in the circumstances he would explain my difficulties to the College, and I would not be re-elected; if I changed my mind before Michaelmas, it would be possible for me to revoke my decision.

Thus I had burnt my boats, and felt that from the worldly point of view I could simply throw myself on Providence. Yet, up to the last week or so, I had such a dread of discussng my affairs and inflicting myself on others that I hardly unburdened myself to anybody, even to Catholics. Nor did I attend Catholic places of worship, except that as the summer drew on I used occasionally to stop at the Cathedral on my way back from the office and pray there in the Chapel of the Blessed Sacrament. The Cathedral had always exercised a kind of spell over me, and I found now in that extraordinary sense of spaciousness which is communicated to the mind by half-lights and by the muffled sound of distant footfalls, a welcome sense of detachment. But I could not yet pray easily; I only asked that God's will might be done, and that he would give me purity of intention.

I said no farewells on my last visit to Shrewsbury, nor on a visit I paid to the Alingtons at Eton, on the last Sunday of the summer half. I had become almost a stranger at Eton ; the war had claimed two of my best friends among the masters ; but I felt there more than anywhere else that what I contemplated would cut me off from the past—the official religion of England, which needs no Test Acts or disabilities to hedge round its inveterate Anglicanism ; the world of school and university, of the worship that hallows national, civic, and municipal life. I might revisit Eton again, but the chapel, with its towering pillars and its familiar rustlings, its memories and its continuity with older days, was no more to be part of myself. Now (irony as it seemed) if I returned to the religion of the Pious Founder, I should at the same time be severing myself from whatever chain of religious history bound my life with his.

It remained to arrange for my retreat. Father Talbot, of the Oratory, to whom I turned at the last moment for this practical advice (for I wanted to consult somebody on the spot) suggested with penetrating

wisdom that the most important thing was to get away
from the atmosphere of controversy ; I had better go
to a French community who had never heard of the
First Prayer Book and the Nag's Head Story—Farnborough was one of his suggestions.   The Abbot of
Fort Augustus, who came there on a visit, testified,
I suppose, to my respectability, and I obtained leave
to stay there between the 8th and the 24th of September, the period of my holiday,

I celebrated at Graham Street for the last time on
the Sunday in the Octave of the Assumption, unwilling
to leave a shorter interval for fear of giving any scandal
to the congregation.   I went home for the following
week-end, and communicated in my father's private
chapel.   The next Sunday I went to St. Barnabas',
Pimlico, and made my last Anglican act of public
worship.   To the last my friends seemed to think my
attitude illogical, and Mr. Whitby, as he left for his
own holiday, argued, " You must be able to show some
reason for going."   I could not give any reason for
doing anything : I was tired out, and unconcerned to
defend my own logic.   It was without hope or fear in
my heart that I took the train on the 8th of September
—I did not then know that Hugh Benson went to
Woodchester on September the 7th—and, as I passed
Vauxhall, saw in panorama the twin towers of the
Abbey nestling under the Houses of Parliament, and
the solitary campanile of the Cathedral.

EPILOGUE

Saevo e scopulo multa vix arte revulsus,
Amissis remis, atque ordine debilis uno,
Irrisam sine honore ratem Sergestus agebat . . .
Vela facit tamen, et velis subit ostia plenis.

I HAVE tried to give a dispassionate account of
many institutions in this book, but I will not
attempt to do the same by Farnborough Abbey : too
many poignant associations are bound up with the
single fortnight of my stay. For those readers who
have the misfortune not to know it, let me say that it
is France transplanted into England. Under the chapel
(unreclaimably French in architecture) Napoleon III
and the Prince Imperial lie buried : *sic transit gloria
mundi* is the lesson of its crypt : it is the place for
meeting your spiritual Sedan. The slow Benedictine
chant had long been endeared to me by my experiences
at Caldey. To and fro amid my strivings and my
resignations move, in memory, the black-robed Benedictine Fathers with their gracious silences and busy
life of prayer.

People who read books of this kind usually expect
the author to answer the question : " Why did you
become a Roman Catholic ? " I must distinguish
(after the tradition of my Oxford upbringing) with the
answer " It depends what you mean by Why." If you

238

ask of a friend " Why did he marry that woman ? "
you may mean " Why did he marry at all ? " or " Why
did he choose that wife ? " ; you may mean " Why
did he fall in love with her ? " or " Why did he not fall
out of love with her ? " or simply " Why did he lead her
to the altar ? "   Similarly, in this case, you may be
asking me " Why did you not remain an Evangelical ? "
or " Why did you not remain a High Churchman ? "
or " Why did you not remain an extreme Sacramentalist ? " or you may mean " Why did you adopt
Catholicism rather than any other religion ? " or " Why
did you adopt a religion at all ? "

These last two questions would involve a series of
handbooks, and I am afraid I must leave them out of
consideration.   At no time of my life have I desired
anything else in the way of religion than membership
in the body of people which Jesus Christ left to succeed Him when He was taken up from our earth.
Until the age of fifteen I believed (without troubling
myself with much speculation) in the Blessed Trinity,
the Incarnation, the Life, Death, Resurrection, and
Ascension of our Saviour, Heaven, Hell, and the forgiveness of our sins only through the atoning merits of
the Precious Blood. I have never ceased to believe in
these things, though later I experienced general temptations against the Faith, and found my way to the
combating of them. At Eton I learned to value other
doctrines besides—the idea of a continuous ministry
unifying the long series of Church history, of special
graces attached to various Sacraments and sacra-
mentals ; I learned to think of Church traditions as

possessing a special claim on the Christian's obedience, of beauty and mystery, expressed in outward show, as part of the natural atmosphere in which a man worships his God. I have never ceased to believe in these things. At Oxford I learnt more definitely to attach a miraculous (that is, what unbelievers call a "magical") efficacy to the Sacrament of Holy Eucharist; to approach and ask the aid of God's Saints as my friends and patrons; to assert the endowment of his Mother with special and excellent gifts; to think of the Bishops of Rome as the successors to Peter's position among his fellow apostles and as the first Bishop of Christendom. Later, I came to regard the Bishop of Rome not merely as the Primate, but the natural administrative Head and doctrinal Teacher of Christians, however much historical circumstances might cut me off from his communion. I have never ceased to believe in these things. So far as religion goes, I do not know that I ever actually ceased to believe in anything.

But, during those two years and more of spiritual exile I did come to wonder whether I had a right to believe in anything—to believe, that is, without being in visible Communion with that one visible Body of faithful people of whom the prophet foretold, " All thy people shall be taught of God." For authority played a large part in my belief, and I could not now find that any certain source of authority was available outside the pale of the Roman Catholic Church. Once inside, I should not care how the authority came to me ; I did not crave for infallible decrees ; I wanted to be certain I belonged to that Church of which Saint Paul said proudly, " We have the Mind of Christ." I was by this time unable to believe that I was already in the Church—it was not that I had ceased to believe any-thing, but that I had a more exacting idea of what " being inside the Church " meant. Now, either I must accept this fuller idea, with all the corollaries it involved in the way of spiritual submission and worldly resignation, or I must give up all positive basis for my religion.

This was the alternative I tried to state to the Father Abbot as I went for a walk with him on my first Sunday afternoon. I think he regarded it as a sign of the rather volatile temperament, and, so far from trying to entice me into the Church (as Catholic priests are often accused of doing) he dwelt again and again on the solemnity of the step I was taking : " It must be for always." I arranged my rule of life for the retreat with his approval; it involved about five hours a day spent in prayer, and one or two more in study ; the rest was at my disposal (after all, it was my holiday). For my study, he suggested Bossuet's *Variations of Protestantism ;* for my meditations, the *Imitation of Christ.* There was certainly nothing ultramontane about my authors during that fortnight ; and, in my meditations at least, there was certainly nothing con-troversial.

My feeling was this. I had by now become so tired with my buffeting against the waves of difficulty that I hardly knew whether I believed in anything ; whether I must not embrace my second alternative, and give up

R

asserting supernatural religion altogether. That first Sunday morning, for example, I read some chapters of Faber's *Creator and Creature*, and my spiritual appetite seemed to revolt against it. "That," I told myself, "is the real trouble: it is not the Pope, or Indulgences, or Infallibility: you do not really believe in God as the Catholics do. If you can steadily face all this mountain of assertion about the greatness of God in comparison with man, you may be a Catholic yet—but can you?" Now, my retreat should be my *experimentum crucis*. If my acts (of resignation especially) during my retreat should result, as they well might, in revulsion from the whole thought of religion, then, for this time at least, I would own myself defeated. But if in the making of them I found that religion was still a real world to me, that my soul still functioned (after two years of vague aspiration and spiritual numbness) as a soul made to serve its Creator and to no other end, then it was all right. Then I would enter the Kingdom of Heaven as a little child; it was close to my hand.

Well before the end of my first week, I knew that grace had triumphed. I neither expected nor received any sensible supernatural illumination: I did not have to take my spiritual temperature, "evaluate" my "experiences," or proceed in any such quasi-scientific manner. I turned away from the emotional as far as possible, and devoted myself singly to the resignation of my will to God's Will. *Attulit et nobis aliquando optantibus aetas Adventum auxiliumque Dei;* in the mere practice of religion, in the mere performance of these (very informal) exercises, I knew that it was all right.

I am not trying to explain it, but I must try to illustrate it by an example. It was as if I had been a man homeless and needing shelter, who first of all had taken refuge under a shed at the back of an empty house. Then he had found an outhouse unlocked, and felt more cheerfulness and comfort there. Then he had tried a door in the building itself, and, by some art, found a secret spring which let you in at the back door ; nightly thenceforward he had visited this back part of the house, more roomy than anything he had yet experienced, and giving, through a little crack, a view into the wide spaces of the house itself beyond. Then, one night, he had tried the spring, and the door had refused to open. The button could still be pushed, but it was followed by no sound of groaning hinges. Baffled, and unable now to content himself with shed or outhouse, he had wandered round and round the house, looking enviously at its frowning fastnesses. And then he tried the front door, and found that it had been open all the time.

That is a very crude allegory, and not meant to represent the actual facts—merely to give some idea of the extraordinary feeling, partly of relief, and partly of incredible stupidity in the past, which accompanied my discovery. I told the Father Abbot that I felt quite certain, but, to test myself, would wait till Tuesday before I definitely asked to be received. From twelve till one on Tuesday I was in the chapel, asking the Holy Spirit to show me my error if I had let any wrong motive or false calculation mislead me. All through the midday meal I was conscious of little except a strong desire to laugh—not hysterically, but in sheer happiness at feeling the free exercise of my spiritual faculties. After the meal, I asked the Father Abbot to write to the Bishop, and arrange for my reception on the Saturday.

During those last few days, I did ask one or two questions of Father Conway, the acting guest-master, not with any desire of " making terms " for my conscience, but merely to set my mind at rest and persuade myself that I had not underestimated one or two claims of the Catholic religion. During my leisure time I read a few Catholic novels, especially *Come Rack! Come Rope!* Hugh Benson, who had set my feet on the way towards the Church, watched over my footsteps to the last. I also rendered into elegiacs—for I knew no such recreation for the mind as this—Crashaw's poem (of something more than sixty lines) urging the Countess of Denbigh to make up her mind and embrace the Catholic Faith. In the two days before my reception I wrote some fifty letters or post-cards announcing to my friends the step I was taking. I had not time to write to everybody, and, since an unauthorized note appeared in the *Tablet* announcing my reception a day before it happened, I saw no further opportunity of personal statements. Most of the letters were to Anglicans, and the dismal consciousness of spiritual parting which the exercise involved quite robbed me of the momentary feeling of exaltation I had experienced, without in the least shaking my purpose.

To Father Martindale I simply gave a reference to a line in the Sixth Book :

Jam tandem Italiae fugientis prendimus oras.

I finished the Aeneid the night before I was received.

The ceremony itself I went through (as is the way of nervous people) in a state of something like mental torpor, which did not wear off until late in the afternoon. Of the radiant kindness with which the Community treated me (they had been told the night before) I need not speak, unless to say that of all languages French is the language to be congratulated in.

Among the numerous letters I received there was only one, and that from a stranger apparently of eccentric mentality, which suggested the least vestige of ill-will. The kindly welcome given me by Catholics, mostly unknown to me, seemed all the more undeserved because Anglicans treated me so generously, and showed so little sign of allowing my religious change to make any difference in their personal attitude towards me. In one or two of the Anglican letters one could, reading between the lines, detect a trace of *laetata est Aegyptus in profectione eorum, quia incubuit limor eorum supra eos ;* if the impression was justified, I have no reason to complain, for, after all, I know now that as an Anglican I was trying to force God's Hand. I had this reward for my long period of troubled waiting—that even friends who strongly disagreed with me could see I had been in desperate straits, and could rejoice at whatever light had been given me in relief of my darkness.

In return, what can I wish them but the greatest of God's earthly blessings—the consciousness of doing His Will ?

PROLOGUE

Quisquis es, amissos hinc jam obliviscere Graios
Noster eris.

I SUPPOSE it is inevitable that, after the question
" Why did you become a Roman Catholic ? "
Anglicans and others should proceed to the question
" What does it feel like ? " In answer to this, I can
register one impression at once, curiously inconsistent
with my preconceived notions on the subject. I had
been encouraged to suppose, and fully prepared to find,
that the immediate result of submission to Rome
would be the sense of having one's liberty cramped
and restricted in a number of ways, necessary no
doubt to the welfare of the Church at large, but galling
to the individual. The discouragement of criticism
would make theology uninteresting, and even one's
devotions would become a feverish hunt after indulgences (this latter bogey is one sedulously presented
to the would-be convert by Anglican controversialists).

As I say, I was quite prepared for all this : the
curious thing is that my experience has been exactly the
opposite. I have been overwhelmed with the feeling of
liberty—the glorious liberty of the sons of God. I am
speaking for myself, but I fancy not only for myself,
when I say that as an Anglican I was for ever bothering
about this and that detail of correctness—was this

doctrine one that an Anglican could assert as of faith ?
Was this scruple of conscience one to be encouraged
or to be fought ? And, above all, was I right ? Were
we all doing God's Will ? or merely playing at it ?
Now, this perpetual Is-my-hat-straight sort of feeling
is one that had become so inveterate with me as an
Anglican that I had ceased to be fully conscious of it ;
just in the same way you can carry a weight so long
that you cease to feel it ; instead, you feel an outburst
of positive relief when it is withdrawn. The suppressed
uncertainty of mind was like a dull toothache that had
been part of my daily experience : when I woke up
from the gas, I felt, not the loss of a pain, but an actual
pleasure in the place where the tooth ought to be.
Most people know that feeling, a wild desire to congratulate the dentist.

Or, to take another illustration (for I cannot forbear
to multiply them, so anxious am I to insist on this new
experience), anybody who smokes a pipe will know
what it is to be invited to smoke in a drawing-room.
At first you become conscious of all the difficulties :
the matches are of wax, and inadequate in number ;
there is no projecting flange of the mantelpiece which
invites you to knock out your pipe, no hat-pin at hand
to scour it with ; the ashes you leave and the burnt
matches mount up in a hideous pile which you can
find no machinery to destroy. You have recourse to
desperate subterfuges, until at last you get accustomed
to the uncongenial surroundings, and settle down to
them. But, once back in the smoking-room—what an
orgy of liberty ! I used once to define " home " as

" a place where you can put your feet on the mantelpiece," and I am not sure it is a bad description. That
is the sense in which, especially, I felt that I had
" come home." Anglicanism (or some part of it) had,
like a kind hostess, invited me to " make myself at
home," it was " Liberty Hall " :

Hic quaerite Trojam;
Haec domus est, inquit, vobis,

and it was not till I became a Catholic that I became
conscious of my former homelessness, my exile from
the place that was my own :

Hae nobis propriae sedes : hinc Dardadus ortus;
Huc repetit.

It was not that, as an Anglican, I had been over-
scrupulous about other people's disapproval : I always
rather enjoyed being disapproved of. It was simply
that I now found ease and naturalness, and stretched
myself like a man who has been sitting in a cramped
position.

" But," I shall be asked, " what do you now make of
Anglicanism, and of your Anglican career ? " It is
not a particularly easy question to answer, but at least
some misrepresentations may be worth the avoiding.
I do think that I was called by God to minister to Him
in the office of a priest ; that I went about it the best
way I knew, and was solemnly set apart as a religious
person by a Body which had every human authority
to do so, but lacked the spiritual qualification which
is to me all-important, the direct inheritance of the
Apostolic mission. The simplest way to put it is that,

so far as orders go, I feel about the Church of England exactly what the Rev. R. J. Campbell (in his *Spiritual Pilgrimage*) says about his earlier ordination. As to the Sacraments I received, I feel as if I had in the past made a large number of spiritual Communions in circumstances where, for practical purposes, I was debarred from communicating sacramentally; that, consequently, if and in so far as I was in a position to receive grace at all, such grace was then given to me as is given in Spiritual Communion—I might have done the same if I had passed fourteen years of my life on a desert island. I have no sense of spiritual poverty—except such as we must all have.

For the Church of England as an institution, my chief feeling is one of unbounded gratitude to God for having been born in circumstances where I had a schoolmaster to bring me to Christ. Or rather (for "schoolmaster" is too cold a term) I feel as if I had been left in charge of a foster-mother, who reared me as her own child. Was it her fault if, in her affection for me, she let me think I *was* her own child, and hid from me my true birth and princely destiny? I have no word of complaint to make of any rough usage: rather, if anything, she gave me too much liberty, and let me put on airs when I had no right to. And if at last I have found my true parentage, as I now think it, can I forget the kindnesses she showered on me, her care and my happiness in her arms? Such is not my intention; God forgive me if through any fault of mine it should become my act.

"And so," they go on, "you have found peace?"

Certainly I have found harbourage, the resting-place which God has allowed to His people on earth,

Immotamque coli dedit, et contemnere ventos;

despising the winds, not because no breath of air ever comes there, but because God himself has entrusted the command of those winds to his own Delegate,

regemque dedit, qui foedere certo
Et premere, et laxas sciret dare jussus habenas.

I do not expect to escape temptations against the faith, such as the imperfect soul is bound to encounter and I have often encountered in the past. Nor do I feel cabined and cramped because intellectual speculation is now guided and limited for me by actual authority, as it has been hitherto by my own desire for orthodoxy. I find in the Church *pacem veri nominis, quam mundus dare non potest, tranquillitatem scilicet ordinis;* I do not see how it can be unchristian to desire that.

But if by "finding peace" you mean being laid up on a shelf and, like the housemaid of the epitaph, "doing nothing for ever and ever," if you mean a sort of senile decay of the faculties, and a fatuous complacency in the existing order of things,

Nam mihi parta quies, omnisque in limine portus,

then I no longer assent : then, like the irritated gentleman when a complete stranger asked him if he had found peace, I must answer "No ! I've found War !" Did I find, as the days of my hesitation drew to an end, the Church of Rome a smug, respectable institution much lauded by men of the world ? Did I, in my

morning paper, find fulsome paragraphs telling me of
the debt we all owed to the Vatican for its admirable
broad-mindedness ?

Rather, if there was a wrong motive (for all political
motives to religious action are wrong) which then
encouraged me to join the Church, it was that I found
the Church, as in the days of the Apostles, "a sect
that is everywhere spoken against." I found that
Catholicism in Italy was condemned as denationalized,
Catholicism in Germany for its nationalism, Catholicism
in Switzerland because it was pacificist, Catholicism in
France because it was chauvinist, Catholicism in Spain
as a pillar of reaction, Catholicism in Ireland as a hot-
bed of revolution. I found that the imperialist Press,
both in England and in Germany, anathematized the
Holy Father's interference, now because he was trying
to secure the winning side in its ill-gotten gains, now
because he was trying to save the losing side from
defeat. That its influence should react differently in
different environments was what I should have expected of the City which was built to be the world's
centre,

Septemque una sibi muro circumdedit arces ;

but what did it all mean, this chorus of dissatisfaction ?

In the first place, it must mean that the Church was
something big, something significant.

Πρὸς γὰρ τὸν ἔχονθ' ὁ Φθόνος ἕρπει

—divine or diabolical, it must have some importance in the world, to evoke such antipathy. And
in the second place, it had resolute and sworn

enemies. The manifestations of its activity might differ, and the limits within which its influence could be traced might be narrower than many people thought, but still it had some effect, and the effect roused the world to fury. Disagreements there might be between various sections of the Church—and its critics, Heaven knows, have made the most of them—but at least it had one thing in common everywhere, common enemies. They might respect it for the moment, but in the years to come they would not be slow to join in assailing it, the indifferent, the baffled seekers after a sign, the fanatical opponents—as once before, Pilate and Herod and Caiaphas—sinking their differences in a joint attack upon this defenceless but never insignificant foe. Surely such a cause was worthy of being championed. Whatever else the Church might give or deny me, she could not refuse me a man's job.

Now, as I say, if such motives swayed me, they were wrong. It is cowardly to join the Church just because the Church is large, or influential : I had often had the argument put to me, and rejected it :

> They are slaves, who dare not be
> In the right with two or three.

And it is wrong to join the Church because the Church seems to you to lack support which you can give. You must come, not as a partizan or as a champion, but as a suppliant for the needs in your own life which only the Church can supply—the ordinary, daily needs, *litus innocuum, et cunctis auramque undamque patentem.*

You must join the Church as a religion, not as a party or as a clan. But if I am asked whether I find peace in being a Catholic—does it look like it ? Rather it seems to me that in the disintegration of the world, and of Europe in particular (far greater, perhaps, than we yet realize) which must follow the war, men will look for guidance to the two institutions which override the boundaries of country—International Socialism and the Catholic Church. And the forces of disintegration which will be at work will be in conflict most of all with the latter institution, because, being more centralized, it will be at once more formidable and more vulnerable. To feel every stab the Church feels, to rejoice in the triumphs she celebrates, that should be enough to keep a man's interests active, and his heart awake.

If it were true, as the poet says (but the poet, being a Catholic, knows better), that

> From quiet lanes and first beginning
> Out to the undiscovered ends,
> There's nothing worth the wear of winning,
> But laughter and the love of friends—

then indeed I might find that the world had grown smaller for me ; friends are lost by drifting away as well as by parting, and you circumscribe your opportunities for laughter when the way is made clear for you to embrace the Obvious Religion. " He was simply snuffed out like a candle "—so the world says of the convert—" became quite ordinary, never did anything again." But even the poor buffoon has a soul to save ; God at least has something for me to do, and all the more because He has borne with me so

much, and waited for me so long. And if there must
be grey days (do I not know them already ? And who
should complain of a short honeymoon after a long
engagement ?) when striving seems laborious and
ungrateful ; if at any time some treacherous regret
should look back wistfully towards the years of more
unfettered activity, " no triumphs like those "—well,
after all, one has to grow up sooner or later, and I will
not blame my religion for it. Meanwhile, I have
called this chapter " Prologue," because it is never
too late to have a prologue while you are in his service
who says, *Ecce nova facio omnia*.

INDEX